Dry

twas

Academy of Sciences for the Developing World

Dry
Life without water

Ehsan Masood
Daniel Schaffer

Editors

Harvard University Press

Cambridge, Massachusetts, and London, England • 2006

Library of Congress Cataloging-in-Publication Data
Dry : life without water / editors, Ehsan Masood and Daniel Schaffer.
p. cm. Includes index.

ISBN 0-674-02224-6 (alk. paper)
1. Human ecology—Arid regions. 2. Desert ecology—Arid regions.
3. Indigenous peoples—Ecology—Arid regions. 4. Water-supply—Arid
regions. 5. Water and civilization—Arid regions. 6. Water resources
development—Arid regions. 7. Desert reclamation—Arid regions.
8. Desert resources development—Arid regions. 9. Arid regions—
Environmental conditions. I. Masood, Ehsan. II. Schaffer, Daniel,
1950-GF55.D78 2006304.2'5—dc22

2005029424

Dry: life without water produced by Here+There

Designer: Caz Hildebrand
Picture Editor: Lily Richards
Copy Editors: Barbara Kiser, Peter Tallack
Editorial Assistant: Max Hildebrand
Indexer: Hilary Bird

www.hereandtheregroup.com

Printed in China by Imago

Contents

"Sunshine all the time makes a desert."

Dry environments are, in many ways, a developing world concern. That is because arid and semi-arid lands are most prominent among those living in the southern hemisphere, and have the most impact on daily living there. But in an increasingly interdependent world, local problems become global ones.

As Prime Minister of Jordan, I know that 5 million Jordanians live in dry environments, which shape not only how they live, but their culture as well. Their experience, moreover, is shared by some one billion people worldwide who also find themselves living in the arid and semi-arid environs that cover no less than 40 percent of the earth's surface.

Dry environments have gained increasing recognition as critical – indeed irreplaceable – ecosystems not only because of their austere and compelling beauty but also because they are home to a wealth of biological diversity. Such diversity enriches our global ecosystems and serves as a largely untapped treasure trove of natural products and services.

I began my career in science as a plant physiologist and biochemist. Later, I led the agricultural ministry in Jordan and held the position of Deputy Director General of the United Nations Educational, Scientific and Cultural Organization (UNESCO), based in Paris.

As a result, I know first-hand that dry lands offer scientific challenges comparable to those found in tropical and temperate environments. These challenges are undoubtedly great

Foreword

but so too are the rewards, not only for scientists but for society as a whole. That is because everyone benefits from scientific findings that help advance water and soil conservation in dry lands, and which lead to more efficient irrigation systems and allow easier access to safe drinking water supplies.

It is for these reasons that I am delighted to introduce this volume, *Dry: Life without water*.

This book will offer an introduction full of insights to the variety of experiences that shape the lives of the people who live in dry regions. It also examines a number of initiatives that have been launched to ease access to ever-precious water resources.

For those who are intimately aware of what it is like to live in arid and semi-arid regions, this book will confirm their own experiences and shed light on the experience of others who face challenges similar to their own.

And for those who are interested in effective policies to address water needs in dry regions throughout the developing world, this book will provide useful examples of initiatives that have sought to make a difference and, by inference, afford a brief compendium of lessons that can be learned and applied elsewhere.

As United Nations Secretary General Kofi Annan has noted:

"The risks of desertification are substantial and clear. Desertification undermines the fertility of the world's land. It contributes to food insecurity, famine and poverty, and can give rise to social, economic and political tensions that can cause conflicts, further poverty and land degradation."

And as the stories that follow illustrate, efforts to minimize the risks of desertification are also substantial and clear.

It is in this spirit of concern yet hope that I urge you to engage with the text and photos of *Dry: life without water*.

Adnan Badran
Former Prime Minister, The Hashemite Kingdom of Jordan

The Global Environment Facility (GEF) is an international trust fund created in 1991 that helps developing countries invest in projects to protect the environment. In 2000, it awarded the Academy of Sciences for the Developing World (TWAS) and Third World Network of Scientific Organizations (TWNSO) the a multi-year grant to examine successful applications of the conservation and sustainable use of biological diversity in arid and semi-arid regions in the developing world.

TWAS and TWNSO are two closely-related organizations headquartered in Trieste, Italy. Both are dedicated to promoting scientific excellence in the developing world and to uncovering research-based solutions to critical problems faced by people in the southern hemisphere. TWAS, the lead

Introduction

organization, is administered by the United Nations Educational, Scientific and Cultural Organization (UNESCO) and is funded largely by the government of Italy. TWNSO, in turn, operates under the administrative umbrella of TWAS.

The goals of the GEF-funded project were twofold: first, to provide opportunities for scientists and specialists in economic development and in public policy to learn about the successful work of their colleagues so that they could apply the 'lessons learned' by others to their own efforts; and, second, to raise public awareness of the valuable resources found in dry regions across the developing world. The abiding perceptions that drove the project were that dry lands in the developing world are not only neglected places where poor people live but are also resilient and resource-rich places that deserve more attention than they have received both from the global scientific and policy communities and from the wider public.

The GEF project was given the name: "Promoting Best Practices for Conservation and Use of Biodiversity of Global Significance in Arid and Semi Arid Zones." Its results were showcased in a series of scientific conferences in Chile, Mongolia, Oman, Egypt and Tunisia where 'best practices' in the management of resources in arid and semi-arid regions in the developing world were on display.

To help ensure that the most successful and authoritative case studies were represented, a worldwide 'call for papers' was disseminated before the first conference and a review panel of prominent scientists, well-versed in the issues of biological diversity in dry lands, was assembled to review the applications and choose the strongest submissions.

More than 75 case studies from over 50 scientific institutions in developing countries were presented and discussed at the five international and regional conferences held over the four-year duration of the project. In addition, two publications were produced to provide opportunities for an expert audience to learn about these experiences. The first publication, *Conserving*

Biodiversity in Arid Regions, was published by Kluwer Academic Publishers in 2003 and included 35 case studies.

The second publication, *Sharing Innovative Experiences: Examples of the Successful Conservation and Sustainable Use of Dryland Biodiversity*, was published by the United Nations Development Programme (UNDP) Special Unit for South-South Cooperation, and included 18 case studies. It was designed for policy analysts and decision makers in the developing world. Both of these publications were subject to the conventional peer-review processes afforded to scholarly and technical publications.

Dry draws, in part, on the material produced in these two volumes. The goal of this book, however, is to reach a larger and more diverse audience – both in the developed and developing world – and to raise broader public awareness about dry regions, which cover nearly 40 percent of the world's land surface (and more than half the land surface in the developing world).

Dry is a testament to the value of team work – between scientists, designers, editors, picture researchers, publishers and writers.

To reach such a broad audience we invited prominent science journalists and writers, and asked them to cast the technical information found in our two specialist books into stories that offer snapshots of what it is like to live in arid and semi-arid places. The topics were chosen in part because they included initiatives, based on the application of knowledge, that have been launched to improve the environmental and economic well-being both of these places and those who live there. The essays in this book, 16 in all, span sites in Africa, Asia, and Central and South America, and the Middle East.

The design and photo research for this book has been placed in the hands of a team that is expert in creating attractive yet informative books that both educate and enthuse a broad readership. The stunning photographs that follow will allow readers to view as well as to read about these places and projects. We hope this book will find a place in homes, classrooms and libraries. Ultimately, we hope to have provided intriguing and insightful information to young and old alike in both the developed and developing world, enabling readers to come away from this book having learned something and wanting to learn something more.

The organizations that we represent – TWAS and TWNSO – have increasingly sought to engage wider society in a meaningful dialogue on the central role that science, technology and knowledge play in addressing critical social and economic needs in the developing world. *Dry: Life without water* – and, more generally, the broad-ranging project upon which this book is based – is intended to allow us to take some modest steps in advancing this goal of making the pursuit of modern science and knowledge and its fruits accessible to the widest-possible audience.

C.N.R. Rao
President
Academy of Sciences for the
Developing World (TWAS)
Third World Network of Scientific
Organizations (TWNSO).

Mohamed H.A. Hassan
Executive Director
TWAS
Secretary General
TWNSO

A dry environment is an inhospitable one. After all, where water is scarce, so too are people. Or, so it would seem. Yet facts on the ground tell us otherwise.

The sub-title of this book is *life without water*. Life of course cannot exist without water. But there is plenty of life in environments where water is scarce.

Up to a billion people live in the dry lands of the developing world. They are invariably among the poorest. Many belong to some of the world's oldest cultures, struggling to come to terms with modernity. These include the Maasai of Kenya, the Chorfa communities of Morocco, or the Topnaars of the Namib desert. Some are among the world's most isolated people, such as those who live in Pakistan's Thar desert, or inhabitants of the Atacama in Chile, where a single landline telephone is all that connects one town to the rest of the world. Almost all will be worse off if their surrounding natural resources are degraded, because it is these very resources, such as forests and wetlands, that inhabitants of dry countries depend on for their survival and livelihoods.

While *Dry* highlights the problems of isolated communities – of coping with and responding to modernity and of poverty – more than all of these it also is a handbook of hope.

Each of the 16 essays is an example of how people were able to overcome an aspect of their hardship, or who saw (even a temporary) improvement to their environment and quality of life through the application of knowledge, or of research. This might have been modern scientific knowledge, such as the expertise contained in Sudan's veterinary clinic for its desert camels; or centuries-old traditional knowledge, such as the conservation ethics of Kenya's Maasai.

In selecting and editing this collection, we learned six lessons. What are they?

Why *Dry*?

• Follow the money

All initiatives that try and improve the local environment as well as the quality of life of those who depend on natural resources, cost money. Of the projects featured in *Dry*, those that were funded mostly (or entirely) from outside sources succeeded for a shorter time than projects which were funded through local means. Externally-funded schemes featured in *Dry* include saving Egypt's threatened corncrake as well as designing and building Chile's fog-catching nets. Locally-funded initiatives include Sudan's camel clinic; meeting the basic needs of Pakistan's Thari people; and the design, construction and management of water harvesting in India.

• Tradition and modernity

Many of the communities featured in *Dry* follow traditional ways of life, often thousands of years in the making, but which are now subject to profound changes. In many cases (such as with Kenya's Maasai, or Oman's rosewater makers), they need to decide how best to respond to the forces of modernization, and particularly the advent of large-scale, commercial agriculture. Standing still is no longer an option, not least because doing nothing runs the risk of losing their traditions to modernity. But in other cases, such as with Sudan's camel herders, or Burkina Faso's tree-planters, it is local people who are stepping forward and looking to see how modern scientific knowledge can be of benefit to their communities.

• Knowledge old and new

Modern science is very much an activity that sits on the shoulders of some of the giants of research from different periods in history and different cultures. Some of the most longer-lasting initiatives featured in *Dry* are those, which either promote, revive or build on knowledge or research from the past. These include the revival of goat-rearing in Brazil; Nepal's elaborate system of sharing mountain water in an equitable way; the reclamation of Jordan's Badia desert; Oman's ancient mountain rosewater industry; Morocco's indigenous Chorfa women's knowledge of agricultural science; China's rain-

collecting cellars; or the conservation of the vicuña in Latin America.

By contrast, the essays from India and Kenya are examples of the harm that can be done when traditional expertise (in water harvesting and wetland conservation) is neglected. And the essay from Namibia is an example of how a group of modern scientists came to recognize belatedly the wisdom of the desert people they had set out to help. Much international development these days is more about listening to what people need, and less about telling them what to do. Of the essays from *Dry*, some of the most successful initiatives are those that took their cue from listening hard to the people they were designed to assist.

• Local heroes
Community heroism is a mark of many of the essays, but in a few cases, it is individual (and often inspiring) leadership that has made all the difference, such as in India, Pakistan and Mexico.

• Celebrating success and learning from failure
Not every essay in *Dry* is a story of unambiguous success; nor does each have a happy ending. For example, investigations show that the giant nets intended to trap fog and convert it into usable water for the people of Chile's Atacama desert did not survive the departure of the scientists who had designed them. The financing had run out and local people, it turned out, were unable to maintain the nets without the help of an expert.

• Serendipity and chance
Serendipity often plays an important (though often unacknowledged) role in research and development. Among the essays in *Dry*, the story of how a casual game among China's railway workers led to the development of a successful scheme to green the railways, illustrates how some of the most effective projects are sometimes a matter of chance.

Two decades ago, the problems of dry countries in the

developing world began to rise up the global agenda, culminating in the United Nations Year of the Desert (2006).

For many years, scientists and public officials assumed that the spread of deserts was largely due to poor management practices and population growth. The solution to halting desertification was to grow more trees, or build earthen dams; everything it seems except listen to the needs of people. This has now changed and today there is broad agreement that people, far from being a source of the problem, are integral to the solution. International organizations and national governments agree that the best policies are those that allow people to adapt to their dry environment. There is less enthusiasm for activities that try to change the environment into something incompatible with nature.

This is why an understanding of the knowledge, skills and aspirations of the people who live in dry environments is so crucial. Their history and experience are invaluable to global efforts designed to protect and conserve. The United Nations Convention to Combat Desertification explicitly states that little progress will be made without the active involvement of local populations.

Our perceptions of the world's dry lands are undergoing dramatic change. Once thought to be barren and lifeless, these environments are in fact teeming with life. Once perceived as places inhabited by resilient but unschooled people, they are rich in indigenous knowledge from which we can all learn.

Dry may take you to faraway places, but we hope you will return home with a renewed sense of hope for the future of some of the world's poorest people, and a renewed sense of wonder about the intricate relationship that exists between them and the natural world.

Ehsan Masood *and*
Daniel Schaffer *– Editors*

Sudan's camel healers

by Peter McGrath

 Sudan has been home to tribes of camel herders for centuries. A new camel clinic aims to improve camel health by marrying indigenous knowledge with modern veterinary know-how.

Six thousand years. That, according to some estimates, is the length of time that has passed since the dromedary camel (the one with a single hump) first came into use as the silent workhorse of the desert. The people of Sudan are believed to have been among the first to breed camels, a feat that gave the Kabashish tribe, in the northwest and the Beja tribe in the east control over the valuable trade routes between the Red Sea ports and the Nile valley.

In the 1800s the Rashaida tribe migrated from the Arabian peninsula and now shares parts of eastern Sudan with the Beja. Each tribe follows its own migration routes annually. Members of the Rashaida, for example, move north during the rainy season (August to October), to take advantage of the lush growth induced by the rains in the desert to the east of Atbara, a city that lies at the confluence of the Atbara and Nile rivers.

In the dry season, the Rashaida turn their camel herds south, travelling some 400 kilometers as far as Doka and the Dinder National Park on the border with Ethiopia. At the center of this migration route lies Showak, 400 kilometers northeast of Khartoum. Showak is the site of a special type of health clinic – one that caters exclusively to camels. The clinic was established at Showak in 2003 so that it could be close to the camel herding routes. It is part of a Khartoum University program designed to study diseases in local camels and to develop effective ways to diagnose, control and eventually cure them.

Suffering in silence

Sudan is one of the world's poorest countries. It covers some 2.5 million square kilometers (roughly a quarter of the size of the USA). The north of the country is arid desert and conditions are harsh – temperatures may reach 40°C during the day and drop to freezing at night. In contrast, more southerly areas are covered with savannah-type grasslands and acacia trees adapted to the semi-arid conditions and sparse seasonal rainfall. The south is also where Sudan's oil reserves have been found.

Two mighty rivers flow into southern Sudan: the White

Previous page: **Camel utility vehicle: Camels are used to transport people and goods, but many of Sudan's camels die from diseases caused by parasites.**

Nile from its source at Lake Victoria in Uganda, and the Blue
Nile from its source in the Ethiopian highlands. They converge at
Khartoum, the capital city, from where their combined waters
flow north through Egypt to the Mediterranean Sea. Most of
Sudan's 40 million people live along the Nile river and its
irrigated plains or close to the country's Red Sea coast. But
thanks to the camel, many tribes are still living nomadic lifestyles
in Sudan's arid regions to the east and west of the great river,
much as their ancestors have done for centuries. Between them,
the nomadic tribes are responsible for some 7,000 camels, says
Hamid Abdalla from the Camel Disease Research Group at the
University of Khartoum's Camel Research Center, who helped
to establish the Showak clinic.

Camels, like all animals – domestic or wild – have their
own diseases, from which a good number die.

The bulk of the Showak clinic's work is in parasitic
diseases. Sudan's camels suffer from many of these, including
gastrointestinal worms, mites that cause mange, and
trypanosomes, organisms that live in the blood and are similar to
those that cause sleeping sickness in humans and are transmitted
by the bite of the tsetse fly. Camel herders and local leaders have
known about these diseases for generations, but their treatments,
based on indigenous experience, have not always worked.

Bacterial infections are common, too, and have been
implicated in calf diarrhea and mastitis, an infection of the
udder that is also common in dairy cattle. There is also the
mysterious 'bent-neck' syndrome, a strange disease of unknown
cause that prevents camels from lifting their heads, forcing them
to almost drag their heads along the ground.

One of the biggest concerns is abortion – or, more
accurately, spontaneous abortion – which is estimated to affect
between 25 and 40 percent of pregnant camels. Few seem to
know or understand why the rates are so high. One cause is
believed to be parasitic and a strong candidate is the worm,
Trypanosoma evansi, which also causes a disease known by the
herdsmen as 'gufar.' Abdalla says that the clinic plans to test
pregnant camels for this parasite as well as another parasite,
Toxoplasma gondii, which has been linked to abortion in other

animals, such as sheep and goats, in other countries.

Blood-sucking ticks may also turn out to be a cause of premature camel death. "Early on in the project we discovered a tremendous number of ticks, including some surprisingly heavy infestations for which we have already begun treating some herds," says Abdalla. In Africa, ticks are a cause of many livestock diseases, so this finding has meant that the boundaries of the research planned for the Showak clinic have been expanded. Among camels, ticks are believed to be implicated in the deaths of 23 percent of adults and 20 percent of calves. Because camels reproduce slowly – each female produces a calf perhaps only every other year – every birth is precious and every dead calf signifies a significant economic loss.

Camelpox is also well known in Sudan and elsewhere. The camel pox virus, for example, is the closest known relative of the human smallpox virus – though it infects a tiny number of camels and is not known to infect humans.

Part of the reason why so little is known about the causes of camel diseases undoubtedly lies in modernity. Since the advent of motor transport and air-freight, there is less use for camels as a means of transporting goods. As a result, developments in camel husbandry have lagged advances made in other livestock sectors such as cattle and sheep.

Learning from each other

Organizing veterinary medicine for the camels of Sudan has been a challenge for all those involved, but ultimately a rewarding one as it has meant that each group has had to learn new skills and new ways of working. Among herders and local leaders, there is little tradition of veterinary medicine; or of working with university-trained researchers. The scientists, for their part, had little practical experience working with people not trained in conventional science. They also have much less experience in the art of camel herding – which they needed to master, and quickly.

"The first thing we did," says Abdalla, "was to invite

Previous page: **One careful owner: Buyers and sellers at a camel market.**

tribal leaders to a meeting in which we explained the purposes of our study." A first priority, he adds, was to learn more about the herds and track them regularly for camel health checks. The most effective method for tracking the herds is one that has been in use from the earliest times and basically involves following camel tracks in the sand. The scientists discovered that each herd contains an average of 50 to 60 animals. Abdalla and his colleagues have had to learn the skill of keeping track of up to 100 camel herds – some 6000 camels.

A second priority for the scientists was to convince herders and local leaders that, in order to understand camel illnesses better, they would need to take samples from the animals for testing back at their laboratories. These included blood samples for identifying trypanosomes; bits of feces for identifying the eggs of intestinal worms; and skin scrapings for confirming the presence of mange-causing mites. By providing feedback about their discoveries to the camel herders, Abdalla and his colleagues were able to build confidence and trust and to devise a roadmap for research that joined their university-based knowledge with the indigenous knowledge of the herders. Ultimately, what they want to do is to pass on as much of their knowledge and skills in diagnosis to the herders, so that they can bring the camels into the clinic as early as possible for treatment.

In just two short years, the results already look promising. Abdalla says that follow-up studies indicate that more camels are living longer; and the clinic is getting fewer referrals from camel owners. "We hope that we are not only doing good science, but are also providing direct benefits to the people of eastern Sudan, helping them maintain their traditional lifestyles."

One hump, or two

The single humped dromedary of North Africa and Western Asia and the twin-humped bactrian of the deserts of Central Asia are two well-known types of camels. But there are many more, just as there are many breeds of cattle and sheep. Animal breeds emerge in response to changes in their environments; or deliberately to serve specific purposes. Cattle are bred for milk or meat production, just as sheep are bred for their wool or their meat.

In the same way, camel breeders aim to breed animals based on such traits as milk production, meat production, strength and endurance, drought tolerance or speed. The Rashaida nomads of Sudan, for example, commonly breed two types of camel. One is called the Rashaida, a red-colored and relatively small but sturdy camel that produces a good yield of milk, has good drought resistance and is used for transport.

The second, the Anafi breed is characterized by its white color, longer legs and slender body. Being able to maintain speeds of 7 to 12 kilometers per hour, especially after the first 10 kilometers, it is also used for racing in Saudi Arabia and the other Gulf states and provides a lucrative export for the Rashaida nomads. The Beja tribe, on the other hand, breed the famous Bishari racing camels that have won many prizes in Saudi Arabia.

Other countries beyond Sudan, also have camel breeds that have been developed for specific uses. In Rajasthan in India, for example, the Bikaneri is a dark reddish – or black/brown camel – capable of hauling loads of up to two tons for up to eights hours a day. It is also a source of good quality camel hair. The pale brown Jaisalmeri is a racing camel with young females reaching speeds of up to 30 kilometers an hour. In contrast, the Kachchhi has been bred for its milk and can produce up to 4.5 liters a day.

Peter McGrath is a writer and editor at the Academy of Sciences for the Developing World, based in Trieste, Italy.

Desertification has decimated
Burkina Faso's forests – but hopes
for recovery are rising as
researchers go back to the earth to
nurture the nation's trees.

Burkina Faso's forest nurseries

by Jim Giles

Previous page: **Swept away: degraded land, deforestation and a landlocked location in the arid Sahel have left much of Burkina Faso a barren, storm-scoured landscape.**

Above: **Now nearly denuded, this stretch of land was crowded with zizyphus, bombax and other native trees just 15 years ago.**

The culinary uses alone sound miraculous. Cakes from the fruit of the zizyphus tree. A savoury sauce made with the flowers of the bombax. Sherbety drinks from the plump green fruit of the baobab. Oil from the red palm. Then there is wood for building, cooking and heat – and, from the shea tree, a smooth butter that can be sold for use in cosmetics. List the uses of Burkina Faso's trees, and the country sounds like a Shangri-La, a plentiful land where nature provides for people's every need.

However, the reality is very different, for often, the desperately poor people of this landlocked West African nation go short of food. For, while it is blessed with a range of natural resources that are rich in potential, Burkina Faso lacks the water to exploit them.

The country sits in the Sahelian zone, an arid strip spanning the continent below the Sahara that receives rain for just three months of the year. Few of Burkina Faso's 14 million citizens can be sure that the land will provide for them.

Yet, in a few farms across the country, things are changing. No one can bring more water to Burkina Faso. But local people, scientists and development organizations are working on how to maximize the potential of the precious drops that fall every year. And the country's extraordinary range of trees is playing an important role.

Nursery network

Villagers are using the latest research techniques to develop a network of forest nurseries, and digging new wells to water the trees. This formerly barren land is becoming dotted with pockets of green that are becoming richer and healthier with the passage of time.

Such schemes find themselves up against decades of environmental degradation. As in neighboring countries, the forests of Burkina Faso have suffered as successive waves of generations of farmers clear the land for crops. Nine out of 10 Burkinabe work the land, and the goods they produce account for 40 percent of the country's gross domestic product. This dependence on agriculture has taken a heavy toll on the local forests. There is hardly a tree to be seen for tens of kilometers around highly populated areas such as Ouagadougou, the capital.

Definitive statistics on Burkina Faso's forests are hard to come by, yet the few that exist present a bleak picture. The World Resources Institute, an environmental think tank based in Washington DC, estimates that almost none of the country's original forest cover remains.

Replanted forest and plantations still cover around a quarter of the country, but this area fell by around 3 percent between 1990 and 2000, as land was cleared for agriculture. The creeping advance of the Sahel, together with overuse of farmed soils, is also creating 320 square kilometers of desertified land every year.

This slow environmental decay is being inflicted on a

Above: **To keep their fledgling tree nurseries watered, villagers make diguettes-arcs and lines of stones designed to catch rainwater and halt soil erosion.**

country already critically short of resources. Almost half the population lives below the poverty line. In terms of infant mortality, a good guide to the strength of a nation's health services, Burkina Faso ranks in the bottom 20, worldwide. Local politics has not been kind either: hundreds of thousands of refugees, victims of unrest in neighboring Ivory Coast, have crossed the border over the last two years.

Yet such statistics obscure the resilience of the Burkinabe. When severe famine hit Niger in the summer of 2005, Burkina Faso managed relatively well. Even in the north of the country on the borders of the Sahel, where summer temperatures hit 50° C and annual rainfall is just 600 millimeters, many farmers still managed to feed their families.

And now, thanks to a combination of local knowledge, indigenous science projects and overseas funding and expertise, the country's agriculture sector is proving more robust than that of neighboring countries. One reason for that is the success of forest nurseries and the numerous woodlands created from them.

Setting the seed

The case of Namwaya Sawadogo, a small trader turned successful farmer, reveals just what can be achieved. Sawadogo, father of 12 and husband to 3 wives, is something of a celebrity in Burkina Faso. Twenty years ago, he struggled to feed his family. Now he sells excess produce at market and is, by local standards, a wealthy man. Government ministers have visited his farm, and the UN has highlighted the way in which his projects combine outside help and local knowledge.

Sawadogo's break came in 1990, when he attended a government course that taught him how to establish a forest nursery. Settling eventually on eucalyptus trees, he established a 3-hectare nursery on family land, leaving enough space between the trees to grow crops such as groundnuts. It was a risk: most local farmers in the Sanmatenga province, where he lives, focus on food crops. Yet the decision proved a wise one financially.

The eucalyptus trees thrived. Because there is money to

be made from selling eucalyptus oil, other farmers were encouraged to buy saplings from Sawadogo. Additional nurseries followed, including plantations of kapok – a massive tropical tree that produces tough, water-resistant fibers – and neem, which has antibacterial and other medicinal uses. By integrating food crops and livestock grazing with his plantations, Sawadogo is now seen as a smart agricultural innovator. More importantly, he is able to feed his large family even when poor rains force other people to buy in food.

Burkina Faso's scientists want to encourage more farmers to follow in Sawadogo's enterprising steps. At the National Tree Seed Centre in Ouagadougou, some simple research projects are helping to achieve that.

Recent work has focused on finding a replacement for the plastic bags commonly used to germinate seeds and transport young plants from forest nurseries. The bags do the job, but cost a few cents each – a significant issue in a country where average annual incomes are around US$300. And because the plastic used is not biodegradable, it poses a disposal problem.

Above: **Planting next to diguettes gives thirsty saplings the best chance of rooting.**

Since 2000, the seed center scientists have been experimenting with an alternative: earthenware containers made from a mix of clay, manure, sand and millet husks. Similar ingredients make up the bricks used to construct rural houses, so farmers find the containers straightforward to produce. At the seed center, researchers fashioned the mix into bowls around 25 centimeters high and 8 centimetres across, and began testing the containers with 17 different species of seeds and cuttings taken from the country's forests.

The results were encouraging, although the containers failed to match the performance of the bags. Germination took longer, for instance – 12 days for the containers, compared to just 7 for the bags.

And after four months the saplings of one species, Acacia, grew twice as tall in the bags as they did in the earthenware bowls. But around three-quarters of seeds planted in the earthenware containers germinated – not far off the figure of 88 percent achieved in the bags. The difference, say the seed scientists, is that the earthenware bowls do not hold water as well as the bags.

Opposite: **Fruits of the forest: in Dandantiri village's Fada N'Goura Tree Nursery Project, prodigious mango harvests are helping local families weather lean times.**

Containers with a twist

The scientists at the center are confident that when local farmers set the issue of slower growth against the savings they will make by using local materials, they will opt for the containers. "Although the use of earthenware containers is not without problems, in most cases, the economic and ecological advantages outweigh the disadvantages," observes Jean Marie Ky Kiléa, a forestry scientist. The team plans to advise local people to focus on the containers for species that are planted on farms after four to six months in the nursery, as the containers start to degrade if kept longer than that.

A huge variety of local forest nurseries could benefit from the containers. In some particularly arid parts of Burkina Faso, homes are so scattered that individual families are starting to develop small woodlots next to their homes. More densely

Above: **Roots to riches: years of careful tending (above) can yield marketable crops such as baobab leaves (below), a vitamin-packed staple of Burkinabe cuisine.**

populated areas feature communal plantations, run by local people with forestry training. But in both types of nursery, a range of indigenous and exotic trees are being cultivated.

Many species are globally familiar. Mangoes grow well in Burkina Faso, and cashews are an important source of protein for local people. Others are probably unheard of outside of Africa. Few people, for example, have ever tasted the sauces that are made from the leaves of baobab and the flowers of the bombax family of trees, which includes kapok. Or the spicy-tasting soumbala stock cube, produced from the seed of the dawadawa (African locus bean) tree. The savoury stock, often served with porridge made from local grain, is considered so precious by West Africans that many use it as dowry.

The products of some trees touch virtually every aspect of local peoples' lives. The broad, sprawling branches of the neem tree, for example, are prized because they make excellent termite-resistant timber. The tree's leaves are used to treat malaria and jaundice. Soaking the kernels in water produces an organic insecticide for use on crops. Or oil can be squeezed from the kernels and used as fuel or in cosmetics. On a sweltering day when hot winds rush in off the desert, the neem provides a shady, pleasant place to shelter.

People-oriented planting

Ultimately, the choice of species for the nursery will depend on local people's needs, says Tony Hill, a forestry engineer who helps run the UK-based charity Tree Aid. The organization's policy is to start projects when local people come forward with ideas.

Some communities, for instance, need nurseries that will produce trees for lumber; others want to build up a regular crop of fruit or to use leaves for manure and the wood for fire. Rather than run the schemes, the charity makes them happen by providing local people and organizations with expertise and funding. The aim is always for the projects to be generated from the grassroots up and to be sustainable in the long term. "It is

critical that people have access to the trees they need," says Hill.

Around 6 millions trees have been planted across Burkina Faso over the last 20 years by Tree Aid. Other donors and the country's government, working through organizations like its own National Tree Seed Centre, have probably added millions more.

"But the numbers are not important," says Hill. "You could plant trees in plantations across the country and not affect people's livelihoods. But a few trees in the right places can make a big difference to a poor family."

Above: **The plastic bags widely used for seed germination, a costly waste problem in the making, could be supplanted by the earthenware containers now under development by Burkinabe scientists.**

Jim Giles is a correspondent for the weekly science journal, Nature, *based in London.*

The Topnaar people survive on the fringes of the world's oldest desert by opening up to new ways.

Innovation in Namibia

by Robert Koenig

Previous page: **The sun-blasted dunes of the Namibian desert remain stunningly rich in plant and animal life despite just a few millimeters of rain a year.**

Below: **Green gold: with deep cultural and physical roots in the Namib, the *!nara* melon is central to shaping a sustainable future for the local Topnaar people.**

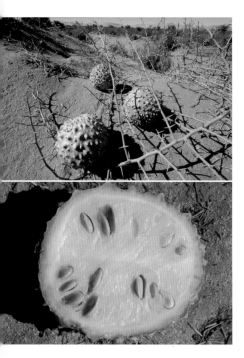

Like vast seas of sand, the shifting dunes of the world's oldest desert stretch for hundreds of kilometers across one of the driest areas of southern Africa. In good years, annual rainfall in the Namib desert is measured in mere millimeters. But the years since the 1990s have been far from 'good' and have spurred many people who live on the desert's fringe to change their lifestyles and livelihoods in order to survive.

The Topnaars, whose community is centered near the town of Walvis Bay, have lived in the Namib and the surrounding semi-arid region for centuries. It is a dry environment but surprisingly rich in species, as well as gravel plains, sand dunes and 'ephemeral' rivers in which water appears infrequently and unpredictably.

The Topnaars are lean, attractive and predictable. They have apricot-colored skin and prominent cheekbones. They speak Nama, which features clicks and a high musical pitch. And like the plants and creatures that inhabit Namibia's dry region, their survival is linked to very light rains and the flows of the Kuiseb river.

"The river is the lifeblood for the desert, as well as for our people," says Seth Kooitjie, chief of the Topnaar Traditional Authority. "For thousands of years, the Topnaar lifestyle always has been closely related to natural resources. We survived by hunting animals and collecting wild vegetables and fruits such as the *!nara* melon."

The *!nara*, a thorny desert plant with an edible fruit, has deep roots both in the desert soil and in Topnaar culture and history. These 'green gold' melons, however, may also help to improve future prospects for the Topnaars as they are integral to a wider plan to improve living standards for the community that includes the development of ecotourism and community-based land and water management systems.

Precious emblem

Over the centuries, the *!nara* has been integral to the Topnaar community. During the old apartheid regime, the Topnaars

fiercely resisted a plan to resettle them away from their traditional lands and *!nara* plants. One ancient chant praises the melon as the "foster mother of Topnaar children." Indeed, a common name for the tribe is the '*!naranin*,' meaning 'people who live with the *!nara*.' The plant has also been used as a medium of exchange – or money. Topnaars harvest the seeds in the late summer of each year. In the past, some in the community exchanged the seeds for other foods or perhaps secondhand clothes and food.

With roots that can grow as long as 50 meters, the *!nara* is well adapted to thrive in dry areas. But the plants are also difficult to cultivate, and harvesting and processing the melons is labor-intensive: it takes as much as four hours for one person to produce a bag of *!nara* seeds. Bakery products, body lotions, jam, juice, liquor and even medical products can be made from the

Above: **A Topnaar girl living in Walvis Bay – a place marked by gravel plains, shifting dunes and ephemeral rivers.**

melon, whose main products are its fresh or dried fruit pulp and its seeds, which are dried or roasted.

"Topnaar history and culture are closely linked to the *!nara*," says Kooitjie. "But some of the traditional *!nara* fields along the Kuiseb river are dying out, mainly because water is being diverted elsewhere."

Disappearing river

The diversion of water from the Kuiseb is now intertwined with the future of *!nara* fields as well as the hopes of the Topnaars.

As the only indigenous peoples of the Namib desert, the Topnaars find themselves searching for new ways to make a living while struggling to hold on to their traditions. Some of the Topnaar's traditional lands in the Kuiseb delta have been threatened by state-sanctioned companies that have been extracting scarce groundwater to meet the freshwater demands of expanding cities and of mineral mines.

Such actions have led to human-induced 'desertification' around Walvis Bay and other semi-arid regions. Aside from concerns about the *!nara* plants, scientists also worry that any degradation of the Kuiseb and its riverbed vegetation might have serious ecological consequences in that part of the Namib desert. This is because the vegetation acts as a windbreak against the southerly winds, retarding the northward movement of the dune sea onto the gravel plains.

"We in Namibia are proud of our beautiful deserts, but we are also combating further desertification that results from land degradation around urban areas," says Mary K. Seely, who directs the Desert Research Foundation (DRFN) of Namibia and is one of the world's leading authorities on the Topnaars.

This non-governmental organization, first established in 1962 to conduct scientific studies, has changed its focus in recent years to concentrate more on practical issues related to arid lands – using lessons learned from desert research to benefit Namibians. DRFN experts are working with the Topnaars and government ministries to develop new sustainable ways for

enabling people to thrive in the dry region. Over the past few years, they have had some success, including community-based approaches to managing land, wildlife and tourism.

For example, the DRFN has worked with the Topnaar community to explain why *!nara* fruit production has declined and to try to improve how the plant is grown, harvested and marketed. Another effort, in conjunction with the Ministry of Environment and Tourism, aims to help the Topnaars and other communities to promote ecotourism.

Desert ecotourism

The Namib desert has been 'hyper-arid' for the past 17 million years and arid for the past 60 million, scientists say. The desertification results from the contours of the land, its latitude on Africa's western coast, and the interaction between land and ocean that leaves little moisture other than morning fogs.

Because the region has been arid or semi-arid for so long, unusual species of plants and animals with unusual approaches to survival have evolved. This is one reason why ecotourism has become a growth industry in Namibia – a trend in which the Topnaars, as the desert's indigenous people, are hoping to participate.

So far, the Topnaars have had only limited success in gaining rights to conduct ecotourism and other activities in the park. Kooitjie says some Topnaars have been granted limited 'concessions' but none has been granted a 'conservancy' within the Namib-Naukluft National Park.

About 35 kilometers southwest of Walvis Bay, the Topnaars have established a campsite with overnight facilities for tourists. "Visitors can hire a four-wheel-drive vehicle and a Topnaar guide who knows everything about the land and the animals here," says Kooitjie. Concessions apply inside game parks, allowing Topnaars, for example, to use four-wheel-drive trails to see the desert's dunes or observe wild animals.

There is plenty of interesting desert flora and fauna for ecotourists to see. Perhaps the most renowned species of the

Namib Desert is the *welwitschia*, which Charles Darwin once called the "platypus of the plant kingdom" – a plant with leaves that stretch into fantastic shapes up to 2 meters long. With some individual plants estimated to be 2,500 years old, the *welwitschia* may be the longest-living member of the plant kingdom.

Welwitschia are just one of the unusual species specially adapted to the Namib's hot and dry environment. Desert lizards, such as the shovel-snouted lizard that 'dances' across the hot dunes, have the lowest water-loss rates of any desert organisms. The web-footed gecko, with its translucent body, raises itself high on its feet to keep its belly off the surface of the dunes.

Although annual rainfall is limited to only 15 to 100 millimeters per year, thick fog from the Atlantic often blankets the dunes to create enough moisture for many species to survive. Temperatures in the desert range from 10 to 25°C. *Tenebrionid* beetles keep their heads down to allow condensing fog to trickle into their mouths. Another beetle, *Lepidochora discoidalis*, builds sand trenches to trap fog.

Mammals, however, lose body water at a faster rate, and have had to adapt differently to combat the heat. Many desert rodents, such as Setzer's hairy-footed gerbils and Grant's golden moles, emerge only at night when the air temperature cools. The black-backed jackals, when thirsty enough, have been seen licking condensed fog droplets off desert stones.

Above: **Surface skimmer: a highlight of Namiban ecotourism, the shovel-snouted lizard hotfoots it across the burning sands.**

Maximizing dryland resources

Gobabeb means 'the place of the fig tree' in the local dialect, and the site of the Gobabeb desert research station in the central Namib originally sheltered a Topnaar village. Today, researchers at Gobabeb are devoting much of their research efforts to deepening their understanding of the interactions between desert ecology and human activities. Native Topnaars are among the beneficiaries.

Because so much of Namibia's protected areas is in the Namib desert, research by Gobabeb scientists has helped catalog the biodiversity of Namibia, which in turn has helped

decision-makers improve land management and develop new types of ecotourism. "In Africa, ecological research has a direct relationship to social and economic issues, such as land use and water management," says the Gobabeb center's director, Joh R. Henschel.

But the center – officially, the Gobabeb Training and Research Center – does not limit itself to merely academic research. In addition to its ecological monitoring projects, the Gobabeb center has operated:

- A project to improve clay brick technology using silt deposited by the Kuiseb river.
- A 'rammed earth house' project that has shown Topnaars and others how to use local materials to build sturdier and cooler houses.
- A fog-collection project, similar to those conducted in other desert regions around the world, such as Chile, that uses a fog-harvesting net to collect water from the fogs that roll in from the Atlantic Ocean some 60 days each year.

Cooperating with Gobabeb and the Desert Research Foundation of Namibia (on whose board Kooitjie serves), the Topnaars have embraced the concept of using modern scientific methods to manage land and water resources. But some of the old ways do not go easily. For example, environmentalists point out that the Topnaars' goat herds and donkeys have overgrazed the Kuiseb riverbed and the green areas along the edge of the sand dunes. Similar complaints have been made about other indigenous populations in southern Africa.

The people of southern Africa's dry regions have much in common and there are some efforts at communication. Even though Topnaars understand only a few sounds of the San (Bushman) language, Kooitjie says Topnaar leaders regularly exchange information with other indigenous desert-dwellers in sub-Saharan Africa, including the San of the Kalahari desert in Botswana and the Namaqualand tribes near the Orange river in South Africa.

Previous page: **Despite their enthusiasm for sustainable management techniques, the Topnaar have drawn fire for overgrazing the Kuiseb riverbed and dune edges.**

Century of change

Life has changed dramatically for the Topnaars during the past century – a tumultuous period during which southwest Africa's people endured German colonial rule, followed by two world wars, and then suffered under the relentless grip of South Africa's apartheid regime. Independence for Namibia finally came in 1990, giving the Topnaars a small voice in the government but also introducing a new set of problems.

A century ago, Germany's colonial government had declared the massive Namib-Notkluf region as a national park, in the process negotiating agreements with the Topnaars. But some of those deals were ignored, and the traditional lands were encroached upon as Walvis Bay became a bigger port and fishing town, especially during the second half of the 20th century.

After Namibia became an independent country, non-governmental groups, working with rural communities living on communally managed land, became important players in protecting the desert's biodiversity. New laws allowed communities, supported by non-governmental organizations, to form conservancies giving them rights over and benefits from the wildlife and tourism activities on specific tracts of land. The goal has been to provide communities with a way of managing their biodiversity while also preventing land degradation and providing people with new avenues for earning money.

While few people have lived entirely in the Namib desert, Kooitjie says the Topnaars – who have lived mainly around the desert's edges – are the only people indigenous to the dry region, and deserve to retain certain rights related to its development.

"Namibia is a vast country with many different areas," says Kooitjie. "Projects that work in one area might not prove to be sustainable in the desert. Topnaars are desert people and have sustained communities here for many centuries. We can help find out what will work in the future."

Above: **Lessons in survival: as veterans of numerous upheavals and the only people native to the Namib, the Topnaar have a deserved stake in its development.**

Robert Koenig is a science writer based in Pretoria, South Africa.

Wetland conservation the Maasai way

by Yvonne Ndege

Cattle are king for the Maasai of East Africa and the task of keeping their herds watered has made the Maasai into conservationists against all the odds.

Dryland existence is a matter of life and death, as the Maasai know only too well. These nomadic pastoralists – the indigenous people of Kenya's Rift valley and parts of northern and central Tanzania – inhabit some of the driest land on earth. In Kenya, this includes the open, semi-arid plateaus of the Kajiado and Narok districts in the south, and in Tanzania, the Ngorongoro and Simanjiro regions to the north.

Much of Kenya may be dry, but there is abundant water in the south of the country, if you know where to look. Strangely for an arid land, wetlands cover nearly 10 percent of the region. These include fresh and saline swamps, shallow lakes, margins of deep lakes, dams, fishponds, marshes, mudflats and floodplain grasslands, springs and streams that are the Maasai's primary sources of water.

Wetlands play an important role in nature. They help to recharge the underground aquifers that supply water for drinking, local industry and agriculture; help to stop flooding and soil erosion; and help to regulate the amount of carbon in the atmosphere, thus countering global warming. Many wetlands are also an important source of food and medicine. In Kenya, fresh leaves from several species of acacia tree are used in the preparation of food, water lilies are eaten during drought, and the seeds from wild wetland cereals such as millet and sorghum are staples.

Ancient ways

For the Maasai, wetlands are a source of water of last resort. They have learned over centuries that when the rains fail, or are irregular, it is the wetlands that can always be relied on. The Maasai are one of the world's last communities to maintain a lifestyle that predates the birth of agriculture 10,000 years ago. They migrate through and sojourn in some of the world's most extreme terrains seeking water, not just for themselves, but for the tens of thousands of cows, sheep and goats they rely on for meat, blood and milk. Cattle, in fact, support 80 to 90 percent of the Maasai, who have become highly skilled over the generations in

Previous page: **The Maasai Mara, ancestral home of the nomadic Maasai, is a remarkable mix of some of the driest land on Earth and a vast array of wetlands.**

finding sources of water for their herds and flocks – including 180,000 head of cattle.

The importance of water to their culture means that Maasai believe water to be a public (or at least a community) resource, as well as a fundamental right that cannot be denied. In Maasai culture, there is no hierarchy of access to water. In practice, this means that someone in a leadership position has no more water privileges than a lower-ranked Maasai community member. The Maasai regard it as everyone's duty to keep water clean, and this is taught to children.

Nathan Gichuki and Jane Macharia of the National Museums of Kenya are among the world's leading authorities on the Maasai. The pair has conducted extensive studies in Maasai

Above: **Passionate about their pastoral traditions, the Maasai herd tens of thousands of cows, sheep and goats-and maintain the wetlands to support them.**

water management and have found that a conservation ethic runs deep in Maasai communities, and that this is derived from their culture and beliefs.

For example, permanent springs, swamps and marshes are seen by the Maasai as sacred sites. Access to such sites is permitted only during ceremonies and rites. Other customs and beliefs forbid any drainage of the wetland, or the indiscriminate harvesting of plants. Community members who fail to respect these arrangements are punished, says Jeremy Lind, a researcher at King's College in London. "Punishment may take the form of a fine, or a curse."

The Maasai believe in the concept of God, whom they call 'Enkai' and whom they regard as the provider and regulator of water, which they call 'Enkare.' They also believe that God uses water to reward or punish the community. "More rains means Enkai is happy with the community and a lack of it means that Enkai is annoyed," says Partalala Ole Kamuaro, a member of one of Kenya's Maasai communities. If, for example, the rains fail, then a sacrifice has to be offered.

Maasai communities divide themselves into what is called an 'enkutoto.' Enkutotos are defined by a set number of families living within a given area and who share pastures for their animals, water and other resources. Before a new family is allowed into an enkutoto, a meeting is held to obtain consensus from other members, who will also decide the location of the new 'boma' or house. No house can be built near a water source or in an area where surface water can flow into a water source. Such meetings also set limits to the number of houses allowed in an enkutoto, which is a way of regulating household and other uses of water and other natural resources.

Other aspects of Maasai conservation include the idea that Maasai need to move between different wetlands so that the land can recover once it has been used for a period of time. Maasai also try to diversify their livestock to include cattle, donkeys, goats and sheep so that no single breed of animal dominates. In areas where water is particularly scarce, rivers and streams are divided into zones that can only be used by people, sheep or cattle – but not all three.

Opposite: **Community and conservation: green ethics are ingrained in Maasai culture and beliefs, centering on a duty to keep the wetlands pristine.**

The clash with colonialism

The history of property rights in the Maasai lands helps to illustrate how the legacy of colonialism in Africa still haunts conservation today. During colonial rule, Britons were encouraged to emigrate to Kenya in an effort to develop commercial farms. The state later imposed formal property rules that subordinated Maasai interests to those of the new settlers.

Under the Maasai treaties of 1904 and of 1911, a number of British farmers appropriated Maasai lands – because these were deemed to be 'unoccupied' by the colonial powers. The Kenya Land Commission, the colonial-era institution governing these acts, created what were called 'native reserves' and developed new grazing schemes and systems for managing land. The net result of these changes was an agricultural system that had little relevance to Maasai needs and which took no account of existing Maasai methods, nor the centuries of Maasai knowledge.

In the 1950s and 1960s, as Kenya's independence from British rule approached, the Maasai began to demand their lands back. In response, the colonial government recommended that land on which the Maasai lived and worked should be divided up – effectively privatized. The government also laid the foundation for a land adjudication and registration program.

Following independence in 1963, a new law, the 1970 Group Representative Act, created exclusive land ownership and rights among groups of Maasai living in identifiable areas. A land title was issued to each group, formalizing its collective rights to the land.

These group ranches, as they are known today, were intended to guarantee protection for the Maasai from further encroachment and appropriation. But this is not what happened in practice. Far from restoring Maasai control, the land was systematically taken by British farmers and others in authority, and over time the Maasai lost access and control over much of it. The Maasai, as a result, had to move and therefore adapt their pastoralist traditions to new environments.

In the early 1980s, Kenya's then President Daniel arap Moi began calling for the group ranches to be further subdivided. While some of the Maasai were attracted to the idea of individual ownership, for others it meant a reduction in their ability to roam and obtain water and pasture for their livestock. The post-Moi era has not led to improvements and the Maasai today continue to face insecurity over their lands.

Modernization and the Maasai

Kenya is developing economically at a rapid pace. Modernization means that wetlands, for example, are now a prime economic target as a source of rich forage for livestock and as a store of fertile soil for agriculture on a commercial scale, which the government is keen to promote. Some in government argue that a nomadic pastoral system like that of the Maasai is unsustainable and needs to be complemented, if not eventually replaced, with modern agriculture. Moreover, they believe that not all aspects of Maasai practice are environmentally friendly. Indeed, they argue that some of these practices are having the effect of degrading Maasai lands.

Livestock, for example, is claimed to be among the biggest threats. In many areas, large flocks of sheep and goats and large herds of cattle use the same route to a watering point all year round, which critics say, is weakening the soils. As a consequence, some wetlands are silting up into muddy pools.

Above: **Horns of a dilemma: critics of the Maasai way of life say the very reason they conserve the wetlands – their flocks and herds – are weakening soils and altering aquatic life.**

Opposite: **Circle of life: a manyatta, or temporary Maasai encampment, is a microcosm of migratory communal life that defies the colonial introduction of individual ownership. After a century of broken promises to restore their lands, the Maasai now face insecurity over freedom of access.**

Organic matter, dung and urine deposited into a wetland as cattle drink is affecting aquatic life and is changing plant types. Another threat comes from modernization in farming. Not all Maasai are pastoralists and some are small-scale farmers. These Maasai farmers are now using fertilizers and pesticides, which destroy wetland wildlife. At the same time, this is making the water for their livestock toxic.

Others, however, see a different picture. Staff at the Drylands Program of the London-based think tank, the International Institute for Environment and Development (IIED), for example, believe that the accusations are unjust. They argue that Maasai pastoralists should not be singled out for blame for environmental degradation, whose causes are complex. They point out that Maasai communities are often unable to present their case to the authorities effectively, in part because they lack access to the top levels of power. IIED staff also point out that many policies that affect the Maasai, particularly relating to changes in land laws, are largely driven by a set of values reflecting developed-country concepts of how to raise standards of living.

There has been some acknowledgement of this view from the current government, headed by President Mwai Kibaki. Despite the push towards commercial-scale agriculture, pastoralism remains an important part of Kenya's economy. Half the country's entire livestock population occupy areas used by pastoralists, and these regions also generate 80 percent of the country's ecotourism revenues. Indeed, the importance of pastoral livelihoods is recognized in Kenya's most recent economic recovery plan which also acknowledges that loss of land is an important reason for some of the problems faced by the Maasai.

Recognition of traditional Maasai expertise is one thing, but the Maasai are also being encouraged to recognize merit in some non-Maasai methods of water conservation. The International Water Management Institute, for example, has been helping the Narok Maasai to build small dams in the Mara river basin. One expert, Malesu Miambo, Regional Coordinator of the World Agroforestry Centre, says that the Maasai are not averse to modernization where the benefits are clear.

The Maasai are an independent and resilient people battling the tide of modernization. Their desire, at base, is to roam Kenya in search of the surge and gush of springs for their herds.

At the same time, all of Africa is changing and this change is affecting the Maasai as it is other communities. The paradox is that with two of the world's longest rivers, the continent in theory has plentiful water; it is just that some communities have better access to it than others.

There is a powerful incentive to keep wetlands, and their regulating effect on the greater environment, in good shape. Appropriate policies and development interventions that can both conserve the best of the Maasai ways while at the same time introduce them to effective alternatives have the best chance of succeeding.

Yvonne Ndege is a journalist with BBC television news based in London

Below: **One Maasai community is building dams to keep the Mara river flowing for their herds – proof that staunch traditionalists will embrace new ideas they believe in.**

Green and dry in China

by Jia Hepeng and Liu Weifeng

Straw tiles, trains and water tanks
are bringing life back to some of
China's driest regions.

"With the moon in mid-air, comes out the old man,
Mountains after mountains he tries to scan
To find water for his family and for his arid land
But after sunset he returns with an empty-hand."

The echoes of this ballad, widely sung in the dry provinces of
northwestern China, describe a farmer's heartbreaking attempts
to search for drops of precious water. The song can often be
heard resonating in the vast Taihang mountains in the
northwestern Shanxi province. It is accompanied by laments that
women don't seem to want to marry Shanxi's sons any more.
The prospect of a life without water, so it would seem, is not
worth even the man of your dreams.

Four hundred million Chinese – nearly one third of the
population – live in China's dry northwestern provinces. In 2004,
nearly 24 million people here had difficulty finding water to
drink. The pursuit of water through every possible means
dominates the daily lives of rural people in northwestern China.
One example is the village of Dangjialing located in the western
part of Shanxi province, one of China's driest locations.
Dangjialing is encircled by mountains and valleys. Villagers live
in houses that are effectively converted caves walled with loess,
the fine-grained particles of clay and silt that travel with the
wind.

The dry climate and high altitude mean that the usual
water sources for rural people (underground aquifers) are out of
the question. Instead, village communities build large water-
collecting pits made from clay in the shape of a jar. These are
locally known as 'rain cellars' and are used to collect and
conserve rainwater that falls during autumn and summer. But
because they are predominantly made from clay, the water that
they store becomes increasingly muddy and unclean –
particularly in the second half of the year, says Dang Jiyan, the
leader of the local village committee.

The pressure on water means that village communities
have had to develop their own rules on how water should be
used, by whom and for what purpose. Perhaps the most
important rule is conservation: that water has to be saved as far

**Previous page: The sands of time
are running out for Minqin. What
was once an oasis along the Silk
route between the deserts of
Tengger and BadanJara is slowly
becoming a desert itself.**

as possible and that there is no such thing as waste or drainage. The top-most layer of water inside water cellars is used for drinking. Water from precipitation is used in the mornings for washing faces. But this water cannot be wasted or flushed away – it then has to be used to feed poultry and livestock. Bathing for most villagers is not just a luxury; it can be a once-in-a-lifetime opportunity, and mostly happens on the day they are to get married.

If stored rainwater looks as if it will run out (as it frequently does), some communities have no choice but to leave their villages and travel on foot for several kilometers in search of new supplies. For the more enterprise-minded, it can be a profitable business. With two buckets balanced at opposite ends of a wooden shoulder-pole, young men set off as early as 4 o'clock in the morning in search of new water supplies. A bucket of clean water can be sold for up to 4 yuan (US$0.50), and a water-carrier can earn up to 24 yuan (US $3.00) for a day's work fetching and selling water – more than for many farming activities.

Rebuilding rain cellars

In 1995, Gansu province suffered one of its most serious droughts in recorded history. More than a million people did not have enough water and some are believed to have died, though the precise figures are still not known. The provincial government vowed that next time the government and communities would be better prepared. As a result, the government launched 'Project 121,' a self-help scheme to build cement-lined rain cellars capable of storing 100 cubic meters of water for each of the province's 300,000 households.

The Secretary of the Gansu branch of the Communist Party, Yan Haiwang, the highest local official at the time, appealed for donations and himself contributed an amount equal to several months' salary. Other government officials and business leaders soon followed and the project eventually won the backing of central government.

Above: **Snow man: A farmer in Huining county in Gansu province collects snow to store in his water-cellar in readiness for the dry summer.**

The tragedy of clay water cellars is not exclusive to Gansu. Elsewhere in China's northwestern provinces, similar moves are afoot to modernize what are an essential insurance policy against the droughts that keep hitting northwestern China. In 2000, the China Women's Development Foundation launched a project known as 'Mother's Water Cellars' across provinces in China's northwest and southwest. Using donations of 116 million yuan (US$14 million), the foundation built 80,000 rain cellars and more than 1,000 small water projects to offer clean water for local communities. The Ministry of Water Resources has also invested some 8.3 billion yuan in looking at ways of improving the quality of drinking water in rural China.

Cement-lined water cellars may not be the most high-technology solution to the shortage of clean water, but they are key to health, hygiene and, in some cases, could be the difference between life and death. Wang Wuzhong, a farmer in the village of Gangjiazhuang in Shanxi province, says cement cellars have the potential to store enough water to meet the needs of families and their livestock for a year. "Now we can wash our faces at any time we want," says Wang.

From oasis to desert

While for some in China (such as Dang Jiyan and the members of the Dangjialing communities) it is possible to survive on tiny amounts of water, others, such as some residents of Gansu province's Minqin county on the famous Silk routes do not even have this facility and are left with no choice but to migrate. The reason is one that is beyond their control: it is desertification.

Minqin was originally an oasis sandwiched between two deserts: the BadanJara and the Tengger. It had long been considered as part of nature's buffer intended to stop the two deserts overlapping into one. But the sands of time for Minqin are fast running out as the Tengger marches towards the BadanJara at a rate of 10 meters per year. As he stands at the edge of the Tengger, 51-year-old Sheng Tangguo says he has watched as, year after year, more of his precious arable land turns into desert. Twenty-six households in Minqin's Huanghui village have fled from the effects of drought and famine over the past 3 years. Sheng's family and that of his brother Sheng Yuguo are now the only ones to remain, but perhaps for not much longer. The desert has crawled into the compounds of their houses.

Not all of the reasons for desertification are natural; some are human-induced. And in Minqin, in particular, desertification has been made worse by two types of human activity. One is the building of a reservoir on the Shiyanghe river in 1958. A second is the extraction of water from underground aquifers. In the first half of the 20th century, the Shiyanghe river was a major source of water for Minqin residents. But since the building of the reservoir its annual surface water flow has decreased from almost 550 million cubic meters in the 1950s to 80 million cubic meters today. This loss of water gave residents little choice but to start sinking boreholes to pump water from underground. During the 50 years this has been happening, the depth of water available for pumping has moved from less than one meter below ground to 200 meters today. Deeper water is potentially more dangerous as it contains higher concentrations of arsenic and fluoride. "This water cannot even be used to feed livestock," says Sheng Tangguo.

Half a century of well drilling has also led to the loss of local species such as poplar (*Popular diversifolia*) and sacsaoul (*Holoxylon ammodendron*), according to Chen Guangting, a scientist at the Lanzhou-based Cold and Arid Regions Environmental and Engineering Research Institute of the Chinese Academy of Sciences.

Above: **A 900-year-old castle in the Alashan desert in Inner Mongolia on the road between China and the West now lies in ruin.**

A water-saving tradition

The story of Minqin is not an isolated one. The neighboring county of Alashan in Inner Mongolia also has a familiar tale to tell. For the past several centuries, Alashan was home to a group of mainly nomadic people. The dry climate and relative lack of

Above: **With household water-cellars running dry, rural residents in the northwestern Gansu province use donkeys to bring water from further afield.**

water led to a strong set of water conservation traditions among the nomadic communities, says Siqinderig Bao, a former Alashan resident for many years who has since moved to Beijing with her children.

For example, when droughts occur the conservation code requires those who have found a water source to share it with others. Similarly, as many households as possible are encouraged to contribute towards the costs of water projects – except for the poorest families, or those who do not have men who can help out with physical labor.

This ethic of conservation applied as much to animals as it did to humans. "In our local belief, cherishing water is sacred. No one has the right to spoil a water source, whether it is a small river, a spring, or a well," says Bao. According to the traditions of

Mongolia's nomads, for example, it is forbidden for livestock to drink from rivers or from natural ditches. Water must be carried home if the intention is to use it for animals. All members of the community comply, says Bao. "There is no police, just voluntary enforcement, because people are afraid of being punished by the gods if they spoil or waste water," Bao says.

But over the past 20 years, these conservation traditions have been breaking down, in part because of migration from desertified Minqin, and in part because of the replacement of camels with goats as the livestock animal of choice. Camels are ideal for dry environments because a single feed can keep a camel active for up to 10 days, which also means that, unlike other livestock animals, camels do not constantly graze on precious grassland; nor do they need a frequent supply of

Above: **Alashan's desert camels in Inner Mongolia. Camels have a light environmental footprint, unlike goats, which are more popular among desert dwellers because of demand from the cashmere industry.**

drinking water. But over the past 20 years, the attraction of breeding goats for cashmere clothing has prompted many herders to kill their camels in favor of goats. Many herders and their families have become wealthier as a result; but, unlike the ecologically light camels, goats have destroyed large areas of grassland.

Greening the desert

As desertification takes hold of more and more of northwestern China, not everyone is resigned to defeat. Indeed, a brave few have been fighting back. One such group can be found in Shapotou in Ningxia province, where, in the middle of the Tengger desert, a successful scheme has helped to green the areas around the desert's highways and railway tracks.

The story begins in 1958, when the Baotou-to-Lanzhou railway was being built through Shapotou. Mindful of the need to find a way to stop the desert sand from burying the railway tracks, the new railway's planners initially brought in large carpets made of straw, which were used to cover the sand in an effort to stop the trains from eventually sinking. "But when a big wind came, we found that our huge carpet was buried overnight by the shifting sands," says Shi Qinghui, a scientist who came to work on the project in 1960.

As often happens in the world of research, a simple, yet effective alternative solution presented itself completely by chance – in the form of a casual game that some of the project's younger workers had devised for themselves to pass the time. These workers had taken some of the straw and wheat stalks and used them to create vertical Chinese characters and walls made of grass, which they then half-erected in the sand. After the winds had come and gone, some of these straw characters and grass walls had survived intact – while the carpets had been completely buried.

Shi says that after seeing that the straw characters had remained intact, the project's researchers began to experiment with making straw tiles in different heights and different shapes –

square, rectangular, circular and diamond-shaped – and then burying parts of these tiles into the sand at different depths. "Finally, we discovered that straw tiles which were one square-meter, with half the length buried in the sand, turned out to be the most stable one in the face of moving sand dunes."

Later, however, something more unexpected happened. It rained (not unexpectedly), but after rainfall, some parts of the straw tiles began sprouting grass. What seems to have happened is that the sand below the tiles had taken on the characteristics of compacted soil and became ideal for plants. The plants were irrigated from a nearby river and some years later, 10 percent of the area around the railway was covered in greenery. For nearly half a century, lines upon lines of straw tiles have helped to safeguard the desert section of the Baotou-Lanzhou railway. The wild grasses have since been joined by trees and the improvement in the soil has helped to introduce many more new species to the desert.

Jia Hepeng is Regional Coordinator for China for the Science and Development Network (www.SciDev.Net). *Liu Weifeng is an environment correspondent with the* China Daily.

Below: **Ecology express: China's railways carry more than people – an innovative scheme has helped to bring greenery to the Tengger desert.**

In a corner of Rajasthan in India, rainwater harvesting has replenished rivers, sparked an agricultural renaissance and brought the forests – and the tigers – back.

Drought-proofing with a difference in India

by Pallava Bagla

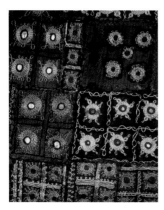

Most of Rajasthan, in western India, is a desolate and devastated landscape. But in the semi-arid reaches of the Alwar district, a new oasis has been taking shape for some years now. In a slow and steady transformation, a group of local farmers in 750 villages has managed to defy the worst droughts in recent memory simply by reinstating their lost tradition of water harvesting, and reforesting the area.

Alwar is a part of the ancient Aravalli mountain range that extends through the part of the Thar desert lying in Rajasthan right up to New Delhi. This is among India's driest and hottest regions, with an annual rainfall of less than 450 millimeters, the bulk of that falling during the brief monsoon season. Many of the villages here were resigned to suffering their way through the searing droughts of the region. Then came 1986 – the year Rajendra Singh came to the district.

Inspired by tradition

At the time a young man employed by the government, Singh had joined a non-profit organization called the Tarun Bharat Sangh (or TBS translated as Young India Association) some years earlier. This Jaipur-based organization focuses on water issues among the rural poor of Rajasthan. Singh's aim was to alleviate the effects of drought on local villagers; his inspiration was the traditional water harvesting methods of Rajasthan's indigenous Minhas peoples, who have mastered the art of collecting whatever little rain that falls on their lands and then carefully using it all through the year.

Since that year, TBS has built more than 1,000 water-harvesting structures in the region, with little financial support from the India government. The technique is simple. At a point upstream of the area's main water source, a semicircular tiny dam is built to collect water from rainwater-fed rivulets in the area. The water that collects behind the dam soaks into a shallow pit, which will then will seep into the ground to recharge the reservoir of water serving the area. This system, locally known as a *johad*, is used in conjunction with good forest conservation practice to keep the soil nutritious and capable of retaining moisture. The result is replenished groundwater and a raised water table – even in bone-dry Rajasthan.

The five small rivers of Alwar – the Bhagani-Teldehe, Arvari, Jhajwali, Sarasa and Ruparel – are all within the catchment of the Yamuna river. Before Singh came, they had nearly dried up. Now they flow year-round. The Centre for Science and Environment (CSE) in New Delhi describes the TBS story as a spectacular victory, and the first time Indian rivers have ever regenerated successfully.

At a time in our history when wars may well be fought over water, this Rajasthan initiative is no small achievement – not least for the fact that the people themselves have shouldered more than three-quarters of the costs. But it has been worthwhile: a study carried out by CSE found that the return on investment in these traditional water-harvesting structures was an astonishing 400 percent.

In Alwar, the main livelihood is a combination of rain-

Below: **The small dams known as johads, designed to collect runoff from rainwater streams, can successfully replenish groundwater while providing much-needed surface water.**

Above: **If groundwater sinks too low, even deep wells run dry.**

Opposite: **Perpetual ponds: the first johad-fed pool built in the village of Nimbi, Rajasthan, has never dried up.**

fed cultivation and animal husbandry. *Johads* are the traditional method of water conservation in the area, trapping water where it falls during the brief rainy months in the ponds or in dammed rivulets. They are doubly beneficial, as they not only recharge much-needed ground water but provide surface water too.

A *johad* will be built at a spot likely to catch the most rainwater. The tanks and other parts of the system require regular cleaning to remove any silt arriving with the water. Too much silt will choke their storage capacity, which is why the slopes or catchments surrounding them must be heavily forested, to prevent soil erosion. Forests also serve as sponges, retaining water after heavy rains, then slowly releasing it over time.

Dammed and blessed

The simple workability of the idea can be seen in the village of
Nimbi. The area had, by the mid-1990s, been in the grip of
famine for nearly a century. Many in Nimbi's communities had
long since given up on agriculture, and turned to making illicit
liqor; or had migrated to the cities in search of a livelihood.

In 1994, with TBS's help, the people of Nimbi built two
mud and cement dams in their village, at a cost of about
US$12,000. These two small dams had none of the glamor or
scale of modern-day mega-dams – at least on the surface. But in
fact, although the villagers had no idea at the time, they were

creating agricultural history in Rajasthan.

The first pond that formed here, after the first rains, has never dried up. And today, there is a belt of intensive vegetable cultivation in the village that is 3 kilometers long – and watered with not a single drop of irrigation. How has this come about? The land is saturated, and water can be accessed at depths of less than a meter. The villagers have dug trenches and sown the seeds for melon, watermelon, bitter gourd and cucumber. This year, the revenue generated by this village from agriculture alone was US$750,000 – and it was the third consecutive year of drought in the area. This is drought-proofing with a difference.

But Nimbi is only one indicator that a working network of *johads* is essential in this arid place. Past mistakes, too, point to the necessity for a sustainable solution. In the years following India's independence from Britain in 1947 many villagers in Rajasthan were overly dependent on the state for their irrigation needs. The state came in and constructed irrigation systems that did not take into account knowledge and experience of local people.

People began failing to clean out the *johads* and left them in a state of disrepair. At the same time, the neighboring hills were stripped of forest cover, which triggered soil erosion that, in its turn, choked the *johads* further. This is one of the main points Singh and TBS make: that stripping the slopes of trees in the region will make water a very scarce commodity.

In the decades preceding the 1990s, drinking water became heavily depleted and cattle died in large numbers because vegetation in the area had long since withered. The villagers lost confidence in themselves, and in the government agencies that were ostensibly there to help. There was a wholesale exodus to the cities in search of work – and the minority who remained faced starvation and struggle.

Alwar became what is called in government records a "dark zone" – an area with little potable water. A short time after TBS began its turnaround in 1994, the government reclassified Alwar as a "white zone"and the seasonal and usually dry rivers flowed steadily.

Wild hopes

Agriculture began to thrive with the water's return. And this wasn't all. Local villagers, mindful of the protective role of their catchment forests, enthusiastically protected them. So, trees regenerated over large tracts of land – and with that came the slow revival of some wild animal populations.

Now, a decade later two villages in the Bhaonta-Kolyala region begun to protect their forests, a 12.5-square-kilometer expanse called the Bhairon Dev Lok Van Abhayaranya. The name was suggested by TBS: *Lok van abhayaranya* translates as "people's sanctuary" to honor the successful conservation work of these dedicated local communities.

Recently, wild herbivores, like the nilgai or blue bull, and India's largest deer, the sambar, have bounced back from near-extinction locally. A migrating tiger has also been spotted in the

Above: **Crop bonanza: saturated soils mean the villagers are feeding themselves and producing enough to sell, even through the worst droughts.**

regenerating forests, and villagers report occasional sightings of at least two leopards in the sanctuary. The villagers seem to bear the leopards no ill will even though there are stories of them stealing goats.

This level of tolerance might seem remarkable, but Swati Shrestha of Jawaharlal Nehru University, New Delhi, has revealed intriguing – and hopeful – reasons for it. Shrestha, who carried out a detailed study of the sanctuary for the environmental non-profit organization Kalpavriksh, reports that the presence of carnivores is actually welcomed by villagers in the area: they believe that the disappearance of big cats from the forest decades ago effectively led to deforestation. The presence of tigers and leopards, the villagers maintain, will inhibit people from going into the forest unless absolutely necessary, and thus leave it intact as their bulwark against drought.

To Singh, the work at Alwar has been a lifetime achievement – and a labor of love. He finds great satisfaction from the level of awareness and sense of ownership and responsibility the villagers display as they restore their natural resources. Today, villagers who might have been busy hacking down trees come up with ideas on how to save their forests. They have devised a set of 11 rules to deter each other from felling trees and wasting water.

A total of 1,058 villages have now built *johads* or other water conservation work. Of these, 90 have been made drought-proof. This means that even if these villages receive less than 80 millimeters of rain a year, they will face none of the hardships of drought. They must just ensure that they stick to planting species of trees and crops that do not require too much water.

TBS believes in the spirit of one-to-one communication and many villagers, having taken care of their own fields, are following Rajendra Singh's example. They are setting out on foot from village to village, inspiring others to help themselves by creating their own watershed constructions. It is a truly barefoot revolution.

Nimbi and many other villages from India's Thar region win on many counts. Their communities are empowered, their connection to nature rejuvenated, and their traditions brilliantly

revived. This is true sustainable development – in more ways than one.

Above: **A blazing carpet of color covers a johad-watered village field.**

Pallava Bagla is Chief South Asia Correspondent for Science *magazine, based in New Delhi.*

The Thari people of Pakistan have battled with droughts for centuries. Now a simple feat of engineering is giving them the edge in their dry land war.

Pakistan's dams miracle

by Aleem Ahmed and Suhail Yusuf

If the people of Thar are asked to name their worst nightmare, most simply say "drought." The region – which straddles Pakistan's southeastern border with India – is an arid zone, not so much hammered, as demolished by drought. It arrives every three years, and may stay put for 12 months or more. But there is a nasty twist to this pattern: the third drought in the cycle tends to be longer and more severe than the first two. The worst, such as that of 1999, can parch the land for three years.

The 22,000-square-kilometer stretch of Thar desert sits in one of Pakistan's remotest corners, outside the Indus River basin – which is the economic backbone of the country as a whole. With no river water to supplement rainfall, the welfare of the crops and herds that make up the Tharis' major source of income hangs on just 50 to 300 millimeters of precipitation a year.

More than a million people live in the 2,300 villages that dot Thar's four *ta'allukas*, an Urdu word for administrative units. The four are Nagarparkar, Mithi, Diplo and Chachro. Nagarparkar, which touches the border with India, was once the most deprived of the *ta'allukas*. Here, living slightly above the poverty line was a luxury beyond the means of most Tharis. Every aspect of people's lives – education, health and work – was, and is, intimately intertwined with the availability of water.

Now life and livelihoods in Nagarparkar are very different, thanks to an ingenious scheme begun by one man back in 1994. That year, Mohammad Khan Marri – a member of a grassroots non-profit organization called Baanhn Beli – started to build small retention dams in the hills of Nagarparkar. The project has succeeded in lifting Nagarparkar from poverty into hope, and could become a template for the region.

Barrenness and beauty

Thar is a challenging land. Entering it, you encounter a world that might easily be centuries old. Its barren plains, with their thorny vegetation and tumbled topography, are interspersed with uniquely beautiful ranges of smooth sand dunes, exposed fossils, and patches of green scattered with round straw houses. Farmers and herders tend to cluster in the fertile spots, raising cotton, sugarcane, chilis, edible seeds and fodder along with buffalo, goats and camels. It it is a marginal existence for most.

"This is the poorest part of Pakistan, where 80 percent of the population live below the poverty line," says Younus Bandhani, director of Baanhn Beli. Founded in the early 1980s by Javed Jabbar – a social reformer and former minister in the departments of information, and science and technology – Baanhn Beli is a non-profit organization that focuses on meeting the most basic needs of the Tharis, including agriculture, education, healthcare and sanitation.

Water supply is obviously an overriding concern for the people of Nagarparkar, as for all dwellers of dry lands. Here, villages emerge out of the desert whenever a freshwater well is dug. But wells, while important, are not seen as a reliable source of drinking water in the area. Most here are brackish.

Rain goes some way towards filling the gap. In some areas, there are traditional methods for harvesting it, such as the *tanka* – Urdu for water storage tank, which is traditionally excavated in the floor of a house and usually measures over a meter square and some 3 meters deep. During the monsoon season, when it rains (although not copiously) in Thar, rainwater from channels outside and the roof of the house is routed into the tank for storage. During dry spells, water from wells nearby is used to fill the *tankas*.

Tarais are another technique for harvesting rainwater. These ponds are built in natural basins by filling the bottoms with pounded clay and rubble; some form naturally in rocky depressions. *Tarais* can be huge. One in the western part of Nagarparkar covers over 6,500 square meters and when full, provides enough water for 2,500 people and 3,800 domestic animals for a year.

Above: **Farmers working the fertile patches of Thar eke out a marginal existence raising a handful of crops along with goats, buffalo and camels.**

Running dry

But rain is a capricious resource. Over the long days of drought, *tankas* and *tarais* empty and are not recharged. Meanwhile, the underground water table will lower with the continuous use of well water. And when the balance is broken, survival can become precarious.

The long, hard drought of 1999-2000 is a case in point. Malnutrition rose among Thari women and children during this period, and pregnant women were put at greater risk of miscarriage, premature birth and related complications. As the quality of well water deteriorated, gastroenteritis and diarrhea spread, causing many fatalities. People had to sell their herds at throwaway prices just to buy food, and the cattle market was saturated with weak animals. There was also a sharp decline in children attending primary school.

Eventually, the intensity of the drought forced many Tharis to migrate, despite relief operations from governmental and non-governmental agencies.

Tharis are no strangers to migration: it is an integral part of their culture, as most of them are nomads who periodically move off in search of better pastures or to sell their goods. Forced migration, however, is a completely different phenomenon and can prove a devastating blow.

When severe drought strikes, the Tharis will have to travel for 10 to 20 days to reach areas with water. During the 1999-2000 drought, up to half the Tharis from this region – some 400,000 to 500,000 people – were compelled to migrate, covering distances of hundreds of kilometers in the scorching sun to reach cities or irrigated areas.

But in this overwhelmingly harsh scenario, there was one oasis: Nagarparkar, the only *ta'alluka* virtually unaffected by the drought.

Regeneration in rock

The Karoonjhar hills of Nagarparkar are a low granite range nearly 20 kilometers long. They are home to some 50,000 people living in 60 villages. In its eastern reaches lie smaller, sparsely vegetated hills. Here, two perennial springs are found, while after rain two temporary streams – known as the Bhetiani and Gordhro – appear. The nearby plains are fertile and very responsive to rain, but the runoff tends instead to flow towards the Rann of Kutch – salty lowlands lying over the border in India. The villagers of the Karoonjhar hills were thus unable to do much cultivation.

As it happened, their environment had a highly fortuitous feature: several basin-shaped plains scattered among the hills. Baanhn Beli had suspected that the basins would work

Above: **Bowled over: dammed on one side, the rocky depressions high in the hills of Nagarparkar in Thar form superb rainwater reservoirs.**

Above: **Weathering the drought: local livestock are no longer at the mercy of the region's vicious three-year dry periods.**

for rainwater collection, but needed someone with the right credentials to test the idea. So in 1993, the organization asked Mohammad Khan Marri – an engineer who studied hydrology from the University of Idaho in the US – to conduct a baseline study with the aim of constructing reliable water reservoirs in the Karoonjhar hills.

Marri recognized the significance of the rock 'bowls' and decided to modify them to create the reservoirs. In some of the basins, the hills stood up on just three sides, leaving a corner where water might spill out. So he just needed to dam the gaps.

The idea seemed stunningly simple, but there were practical issues to resolve first. The villagers in the area were doubtful of the strength of micro-dams their and capability to retain enough rainwater. They were also concerned about the construction of the micro-dams themselves – how much the concrete would cost and where the water to mix it with would come from. A number of searching discussions later, Marri finally reassured them that it was workable.

After research and careful risk assessments, Marri selected a rainwater stream called the Seenghado river, near the village of Kasbo, as a first site. After receiving the villagers' consent in April 1994, he began to supervise the construction. In two months, the village had its micro-dam.

Marri and his team kept costs down by using donkeys rather than mechanized transport to fetch water from the nearest well, about a kilometer away. In the end, the project came in at just 225,000 rupees (about US$5,000) – less than a fifth of an earlier estimate by the provincial Sindh Arid Zone Development Authority, which wanted to build a dam in the same place.

Vision fulfilled

That year, heavy rainfall filled the reservoirs of Nagarparkar, and Kasbo. The villagers, amazed by the glittering expanse of water, began calling their micro-dam "Maya" – meaning "great treasure" in their language, Sindhi. "I was simply overjoyed to see the villagers and their animals drinking water from this dam. That was the happiest moment of my life," says Marri.

The people of Kasbo have now successfully run and maintained their dam for over a decade. "People take care of their micro-dams and see them as a lifeline," Marri adds. Moreover, the project's benefits have been far-reaching. Gradual seepage from the rainwater in the reservoir has recharged wells in the vicinity with fresh water. At some lower elevations nearby, wells almost overflowed.

Before Maya dam, there were 50 wells in Kasbo. Now there are more than 100 – with not a brackish drop in them. Kasbo's great treasure has encouraged other villages in Nagarparkar to ask Baanhn Beli for micro-dams of their own. And Marri has continued to build them in the Karoonjhar hills. Enlisting the help of philanthropists and other non-profit organizations, he had constructed 8 more in the area by 2000. Along the way, in 1996, Baanhn Beli received UN recognition for its work.

Above: **Brimming with hope: the micro-dams have fully recharged 500 wells in Nagarparkar, boosting agriculture and small businesses.**

Opposite page: **Drinking deep: in Nagarparkar, easier times have triggered a boom in girls' schools, and allowed more Thari children to leave the fields for school.**

Wave of change

However small, the micro-dams have brought about immense shifts in Nagarparkar life. The wave of change has been seen everywhere, from the fields to the schools.

Vitally, some 500 wells in the area are fully recharged, and remain unaffected by drought. Now that irrigation is more than a pipe dream, agriculture has taken off, boosting the local economy. The *ta'alluka* now boasts over 400 hectares of irrigated land, and mechanical threshers and pumps are becoming commonplace in the fields.

The blossoming of agriculture has had a knock-on effect on small businesses. Nagarparkar has become an important trading center for Tharis. People from elsewhere in the region will often come here to buy vegetables and fodder, then sell them in various other villages at a reasonable profit. This reselling business employs about 2000 – and that, says Marri, is only a fraction of the thousands directly benefiting from the dams.

With the economic upturn, the people of Nagarparkar

are also finding time for cultivating minds along with fields and businesses. Before the micro-dams, most children in the region were forced to look after the family cattle. But over the last decade enrollment in primary schools has increased at a hopeful pace. Baanhn Beli has aided the process by building dozens of girls' schools in Nagarparkar alone. Shepherd children's dreams of becoming scholars are coming true: Nagarparkar's reservoirs of water are bringing its reservoirs of talent to fruition.

Other non-profit organizations are also following Baanhn Beli's lead. Some of them are developing novel micro-dams from scratch, while others are trying to make existing dams more effective. The Thardeep Rural Development Program, for instance, is working on running small water channels from micro-dams to better fulfill the needs of people living nearby.

For the Karoonjhar hills villagers, having enough water to last a full four years meant the last big drought never touched them. They remain unhaunted by the nightmare that beset the rest of the region. Marri now estimates that collectively, all 8 dams in Nagarparkar store over 4 million cubic meters of water during a rainy year. In essence, that means retention dams effectively reverse a drought cycle for the people living nearby.

Marri is now director in charge of the Drainage Research Centre of the Pakistan Council of Research in Water Resources in Tandojam, Sindh. He provides expert advice to other non-profit organizations on site selection and small dam construction. And in August 2005, government agencies approved his plan to build four new micro-dams in Nagarparkar. The wave of change flows on.

Aleem Ahmed is Editor-in-Chief of the monthly magazine, Global Science, *which is published in Urdu from Karachi.*

Suhail Yusuf is the magazine's Editor.

Think of the majestic Himalayas blanketed for months by thick layers of snow. A dry environment is the last image that comes to mind. Yet for many in Nepal, life without water is not an unlikely prospect.

High and dry in Nepal

by Daniel Schaffer

In admiring the natural beauty of Nepal's surrounding
environment, it is easy to forget that many of those who live in
the shadow of the mountains are themselves very poor.
Opportunities to improve their quality of life are few. What
makes life harder still is that the region north of the mountain
chain is a "cold desert," in the words of Suresh Chalise, formerly
with the International Centre for Integrated Mountain
Development (ICIMOD) in Kathmandu, who has studied the
environment for many years.

Chalise says water is plentiful in the summer, particularly
for anyone who lives near rivers, lakes or at the edges of
retreating glaciers. But winter is an altogether different story.
Freezing conditions make freshwater much harder to come by.
And where it exists, the powerful flow means it is not easy to
collect and then store. Yet despite these (and other obstacles),
ICIMOD has discovered that water does manage to flow into the
homes, farms and small businesses that dot the Nepali mountain-
scape.

Thanks to many years of detailed study, painstaking work
with communities and funding from the Ford Foundation,
Chalise and his colleague Umesh Parajuli of the government
Department for Irrigation have uncovered the details of an
elaborate system of managing and sharing water supplies whose
original designers were local people who lacked advanced
modern qualifications. The system they have devised allows them
to tap into and distribute freshwater equitably among different
communities and among different groups of users. On the whole,
it has kept everyone reasonably happy and conflicts down to a
minimum.

Mustang is on Nepal's border with Tibet. It is home to
some 200 people who live in the shadow of mountains that can
be up to 6,000 meters high. They work the land by growing
cereal crops, tending fruit trees and raising livestock (including
dzopas, which is a yak/cow hybrid). Many also earn an income
away from the farm through the trading of wool and medicinal
plants; and by transporting goods – profiting from their intimate
knowledge of what is otherwise a difficult environment for
outsiders to navigate. The area itself is typical of the region as a

whole. Small villages have been insulated but not entirely isolated and they enjoy a stable self-sufficiency marked by limited but continual contact with the outside world.

Water supplies in Mustang are unpredictable, which means that in order to survive, residents have had to devise a system for collecting, transporting, sharing and storing water that is intended for use by households, livestock and agriculture. The system, says Chalise, is centuries old. It is administered by local community leaders and works well.

Each citizen is issued 'water shares,' known locally as *chyure*, which provide the holder with an entitlement to a certain amount of water. Water is directed via earthen feeder canals from the region's primary source, the Ghyakhar river, to a large reservoir where it is stored overnight and released the following morning. From there, the water is channeled nearer to the villagers through earthen distribution canals from which each resident receives his or her prescribed daily allocation.

Above: **High hoe: Women farmers threshing in Mustang. International aid is helping the district's women to acquire new knowledge and skills.**

A parallel system is in place in Mustang for sharing water intended for use in farm irrigation. Here, residents have agreed to place a limit on the amount of water they are allowed to use for watering their crops. "Each week," Chalise says, "farming residents receive a fair share of the available water for irrigation on a 'turn-by-turn' basis." Upstream residents agree to release adequate supplies of water to downstream residents for irrigation. Downstream residents, in turn, agree to keep the system in good repair and to lend a helping hand for maintaining both their feeder canals as well as parts of the system that do not directly affect their own access to water.

This system of permits and water sharing represents a deal that has worked for centuries. But whether it will continue to work in the future is a more open question. As with many of the essays in this book, modernity represents its greatest potential threat. Modernity means many things. In the context of Mustang it means more commercial-scale farming (as opposed to subsistence farming). It means the flight of young people, who are leaving for the greener pastures of southeast Asia and even the USA. Some villages have lost more than half of their young people through migration.

Modernity also means more tourists and visitors from abroad; and more trade with neighboring countries. Much of this, in turn, entails the building of more roads (to trade with countries such as China). A larger road network will allow more trucks to transport more goods and agricultural produce, and will also allow more cars, vans and jeeps to transport the planned increase in overseas visitors.

Long mythologized in literature and the mass media as one of the most exotic places on earth, Nepal has been an alluring destination for those seeking adventure and spiritual fulfillment. The number of foreign visitors to Mustang, however, has so far been limited to 1,000 visitors per year. This is about to change as the government has realized the value of tourism revenues to its otherwise meager national income; and the ability of tourism to raise standards of living for the poorest.

The likely effects on water of all these developments are several. Taken together, more roads, more tourists and more

commercial-scale farming will alter how much water will be available for local people. This, in turn, will likely affect their elaborate system of permits, allowances, as well as the relationships between users upstream and downstream. The loss of Mustang's young people, at the same time, will deplete the reservoir of people from which the next generation of experts in the design and maintenance of local water management will emerge.

Looking ahead

To address these concerns, the government, along with the Nepal branch of the international development agency, CARE, has launched a scheme designed to improve the efficiency of the water management system currently in place. With funds from Danida, (Denmark's government aid agency), the scheme has

focused on improvements to two aspects of water sharing: the first is to rehabilitate the porous earthen canals, which would help to reduce water loss and also increase the force of the water flow. The second improvement – indeed the major focus of the effort – concentrated on enabling local community organizations to achieve the reforms on their own.

The idea, Chalise says, is to promote self-reliance among the residents and give them the skills and the confidence they need to work unaided. This has meant, for example, organizing demonstration programs on how to conserve water on farms, providing information on health and sanitation; and enabling more women to be equipped with knowledge and skills. "This is essential," Chalise says, "because women usually shoulder primary responsibility for the collection and use of water in both households and farms."

Most importantly, the project organizers helped to launch what are known as community development committees in each of the two major villages in Mustang. Members for each of the committees were elected by local residents and their task was to establish and implement appropriate policies to share, manage and maintain local water supplies. "With such strong community roots," explains Chalise, "the committees quickly gained the confidence of the people they were intended to serve."

The committees soon adopted a plan of work. This included rebuilding weirs and intakes along the Ghyakhar river to improve water flow to the feeder canals, and the replacement of existing earthen canals with plastic pipes.

For now, Mustang is fortunate that it has water in sufficient quantities, despite the arid environment that characterizes this area. And for now the community-based water systems that have been put in place are functioning well. But pressures are mounting as the economy and society confront – and are likely succumb to – the forces of modernity.

As history shows and the experience of ICIMOD confirms, indigenous water systems are an integral part of the societies in which they exist. The challenge for everyone is to see that they can adapt to change and that they are not completely washed away. If they are, they are likely to leave all those who depend on them, high and dry.

Daniel Schaffer is the Public Information Officer for TWAS – the Academy of Sciences for the Developing World – and the Abdus Salam International Centre for Theoretical Physics in Trieste, Italy.

One million people live in Chile's Atacama desert. With little rainfall and no rivers, the answer to their water needs is a three-letter word called fog.

Chile's fog catchers

by Katie Mantell

Imagine living in a land so dry that raindrops are the stuff of dreams. Chile's Atacama desert is one such place.

This narrow strip of desert in the north of Chile is among the driest places on Earth. Trapped between the snow-capped Andes to the east and the Southern Pacific ocean to the west, much of the Atacama is a barren and seldom-changing landscape. In many areas people say that it has never rained – or at least not often enough to get wet.

You might expect such a parched stretch of land to be devoid of human activity. But not the Atacama. Close to one million people live here. Fishing and small-scale mining provide the main means for survival. Most of the desert's inhabitants squeeze into a handful of coastal cities, surviving thanks to water piped down from the mountains or extracted from groundwater reserves.

In the Atacama's many smaller villages, the municipal authorities consider it too expensive to have water piped directly to homes. This means that people have no choice but to drink water trucked across the desert from distant rivers.

This makes water precious – and pricey too. For many, daily bathing and washing is out of the question. The few liters a day that most can afford is barely enough even for drinking.

Reservoir in the sky

High on the hilltops that flank the north Chilean coast lies a solution to the villagers' plight. It is a thick and moist fog that blows in from the sea – a misty reservoir in the sky.

Fog for most urban dwellers is regarded as a nuisance, and is associated with cold, dark nights, and with pollution. In the Atacama and the Namib desert of Southern Africa, however, the *camanchaca*, or creeping fog, has always been considered as something of a life-giver thanks to the many species of plants that grow in places where you wouldn't expect them to. These species are known as 'lomas,' and range from cactuses to ferns.

For centuries, people have noticed how these plants collect the tiny water droplets in the fog. But it was not until the 1960s that scientists started to work systematically on a way to

Previous page: **Net-scape: Giant nets catch the passing fog in Chile's Atacama desert. Millions of fog droplets combine to become water, which is collected through a network of pipes and gutters.**

tap this water source. After years of research, Chilean scientists came up with one potential solution – large volley-ball-style nets or 'fog-catchers' that stand upright on the hilltops, ready to intercept passing fog clouds.

The technique could not be more simple. A fine synthetic mesh, made from polypropylene, several meters long is stretched between two posts on the mountainside. As the wind drives tiny droplets of water through the net, about half get trapped on the net's fibers. More wind drives through more fog droplets, and the small droplets join to make larger ones.

This process needs to be repeated again and again to form a visible drop of water – fog droplets are so small that 40 million need to join up to form a drop the size of a match head. But eventually the droplet gets so heavy that gravity pulls it down and it runs down the net, dragging other smaller droplets with it. Gutters collect the water and a network of pipes channel it to villagers.

The amount of water collected is modest – between about 5 and 14 liters per day per square meter of net. But for communities who have few other choices, it can be the difference between life and death.

In theory, the water that these anchored sails can harvest is almost limitless: clouds bring an essentially unlimited amount of water. This means that in principle, the quantity of nets is the only obstacle to more water for communities. There is never any shortage of fog.

People science

Chilean researchers first decided to put fog-catching theory into practice in the late 1980s. They chose an isolated coastal village called Chungungo. Located south of the Atacama in the semi-arid province of Coquimbo, the village sits on the edge of the *desierto florido*, the spectacular 'flowering desert' when wildflower seeds burst into life after rare heavy rainfall once every few years.

Most of Chungungo's 300 inhabitants eked out a living from fishing, mainly shellfish, in the cold coastal waters.

Above: **Each square meter of net can collect up to 14 liters of water per day, enough for drinking, washing and cooking.**

Surrounded by seawater they could not drink, and with only 100 millimeters of rainfall a year, each villager survived on 14 liters of water a day trucked in from a river 20 kilometers away and from the nearest city, La Serena, 60 kilometers to the south.

Thanks to the generosity of Canada's International Development Research Centre (IDRC), a team of scientists from Santiago's Catholic University together with the national forestry association, CONAF, put 100 fog-catchers on the hills above the village, ready to catch oncoming fog clouds.

Fog catching's simplicity is matched by its economy. The fog-catchers cost just $1,000. The net itself is the cheapest part, accounting for about one twentieth of the overall cost.

The results were impressive. On average, the fog catchers harvested 11,000 liters of water per day – more than double the village's water supply. And, once chlorine was added and the water was boiled, it was safe to drink.

Local people could drink and wash when they wanted for the first time. They had enough water to grow vegetables and to keep a few chickens or ducks. And they could install flush toilets, improving hygiene levels and health.

One resident who remembers how the fog-catchers changed peoples lives is Patricio Piñones, a water and sanitation engineer, who sat on the village's Rural Water Committee from 1992 to 2001. The fog-catchers, he says, had a massive impact on people's quality of life. "To plan ahead, you need a permanent and stable source of water," he says. "The fog-catchers gave us the freedom to think about the future. And for the first time people could work in something other than fishing – they had other alternatives, such as growing vegetables to eat or for sale." The population also swelled as people who had left for other towns returned home.

Pilar Cereceda, a geographer from Santiago's Catholic University, led that first pilot project, and the memories of its revolutionary impact remain fresh in her mind. "Before, women had to wait hours for the water truck to arrive. It never came at the same time each day, so they couldn't get on with other things until it turned up," Cereceda explains. "But once the more constant and predictable water supply from the fog-catchers was established, they felt they had much more time." And they did, as the water from the fog-catchers was carried through pipes straight to their homes, removing the need to lug barrels of truck-delivered water.

Cereceda is among Chile's fog-catching pioneers, yet, like many influential scientists all over the world, stumbled on her field of research completely by chance. As a student of Chile's physical geography she studied the work of physicist, Carlos Espinosa who had worked on a theory for fog-catching experiments in the 1960s. Espinosa saw her potential as an experimentalist and persuaded Cereceda that she should try and put his work into practice.

Novelty drink

Most of the villagers were proud of their novel way of getting a drink. They set up a local committee to organize maintenance of the fog-catching equipment. And the project attracted considerable media attention in Chile and from overseas. Film crews flocked to the village, and Chungungo enjoyed its moment of fame.

Today, however, it is a different story. If you return to the Chungungo hills, you won't find fog-catchers any more. This is not because they failed to work, but because the local authorities failed to maintain them. Fog-catchers are simple to build and run, and last at least a decade. But they need a helping hand to keep them in good condition. It is a simple enough process: the nets need to remain tightly stretched between the poles to ensure that water flows into gutters; torn nets need to repaired; and gutters and pipes must be free from blockage. If this is not done, the system can fall relatively quickly into disrepair, which is what happened in Chungungo. Chungungo's fog-catchers worked well for about seven years. But maintenance was neglected, and the frayed nets stopped working. Then villagers started removing the nets, and using them instead as sunshades or windbreaks.

By 2000, water trucks had started rolling into the village once again.

For Pilar Cereceda, responsibility for failure rests squarely with the authorities. "They could have done so much more to ensure the sustainability of the project," she says. For example, they could have charged entrance fees to film crews or to the many tourists who made special trips to Chungungo to see with their own eyes the large black sails of the fog-catchers lining the hilltops. But the authorities did not do anything to exploit the income-generating potential of the fog-catchers.

Piñones, who still lives in Chungungo, says he would rather blame himself and the village, instead of the scientists or authorities for the fog-catchers' failure. Important lessons were learned, he says, and these will be applied in the next generation of fog catchers, which are to be built in 2006. "It was a good project," he says, "in fact at one point there was too much water

– 4-to-5 times as much as we needed. There were not enough
tanks to store the water in." But he says it failed for essentially
two reasons: strong winds, that damaged the nets; and a lack of
money to fix and maintain them. The people in the village had
excellent relations with the scientists and appreciated their
expertise and advice. "They came to the village to show how to
use water wisely and how to cultivate plants. Local people were
involved. We just didn't have the capacity to maintain the fog-
catchers," says Piñones.

Learning from failure

Given what they learned from this experience, Chile's scientists
are now designing fog-catching schemes that give local users
incentives to maintain the fog-catchers.

In three projects across northern Chile, scientists from

three institutions – the Bolivariana University in Iquique, Santiago's Catholic University and the national forestry association – are building fog catchers with local residents firmly in the driving seat. It is a simple process. Three people can build a fog-catcher in the space of a day. An important aim is to make sure that the residents will not need to rely on outside experts to maintain them once the scientists go home.

Researchers have also discovered that an effective way of encouraging self-reliance is to give the residents a financial incentive to maintain the fog-catchers. In the Atacaman village of Taltal, for example, scientists from the Catholic University of the North in Antofagasta plan to install fog-catchers to supply water to a hydroponics system. Hydroponics involves growing plants in nutrient-rich water rather than soil, to produce vegetables, which can be sold. They hope that if people can make money from this – and so start to depend on the fog-catchers for their livelihood – they will keep the fog-catchers in good condition.

Elsewhere in Chile, fog-catchers are now being put to quite a different use.

The location is Fray Jorge, one of Chile's less-visited national parks found in the semi-arid belt between the Atacama and the capital city Santiago. Ninety-nine percent of the park consists of bushes and scrubby vegetation. But if you climb to the uppermost reaches of the hills you enter a world of clouds and trees. The moist air sustains the forest, which is packed with plants such as mosses and ferns that thrive in damp atmosphere.

The trees themselves are natural fog-catchers – their branches and leaves trap fog droplets in precisely the way that the fog-catchers' net does. As a result, precipitation in the Fray Jorge forest is 1,000 millimeters per year, 85 percent of which is derived from fog. Much of this extraordinary forest was destroyed in the early 20th century, before it was designated a national park. Today, only 100 hectares remain.

Now, Chile's Forestry Association, CONAF, is using fog-catchers to help bring the forest back to life. They have put up 10 fog-catchers, and have used the water harvested to irrigate five hectares of land that have been replanted with three species of tree – olivillo (*Aextoxicon punctatum*), winter's bark (*Drimys winteri*) and petrillo (*Myrceugenia correifolia*).

There is a wonderful sustainability about this system, explains CONAF regional director Waldo Canto. After about four years, when the trees reach a height of 1.5 meters, they have enough leaves and branches to start harvesting their own water. This means that the fog-catchers can be used to irrigate other areas. The system has been so successful that CONAF hopes to plant 20 to 30 more hectares of forest this way.

The forestry association is also using fog-catchers to provide water for goats that graze the foggy hilltops near a village in the region of Coquimbo. CONAF planted bushes up on the hills, but villagers who live down below were unable to graze their livestock without water for their animals. Now, two fog-catchers together provide more than 140 liters of water a day – enough water for 50 goats. Canto estimates that as a result, villagers' incomes have risen by almost a third.

These different projects reveal the versatility of fog-catchers, he says. "In the case of the forest of Fray Jorge, the contribution of fog-catchers is to science; in Chungungo, it was for the health of the people; in this case, it is for livestock and the economic well-being of the people."

And there are many other, as yet untapped, ways in which this technology could be used to sprinkle life into Chile's arid zones, Canto says. For example, many spectacular beaches along Chile's 4,000 kilometer-long coastline are empty of tourists – simply because there is no drinking water. Maybe fog-catchers could be the answer. And they could also provide a cost-effective way to provide water to enable the mining of mineral deposits that have not yet been exploited.

It is not just the Chileans that have recognized this potential. Fog-catchers have popped up in many of the world's dry spots, including the Canary Islands, Namibia, Nepal and Peru, helping to increase vital water supplies for people, plants and animals. Economic welfare, environmental vitality, community health and cultural values have all benefited as a result. They are certainly one ingenious solution to the water-stress that comes from living in the driest places on Earth.

Katie Mantell is a freelance writer based in London and has worked as a journalist in Chile.

The village of Pilar in northeastern Brazil was scheduled to die along with the local copper mining industry. Then it took a second look at the animals roaming its streets...

New life for Brazil's goat town

by Marcelo Leite

The village of Pilar with few adjustments, is straight out of a novel from the "magic realism" school of Latin American literature. Never mind the fact that it's not a town in its own right, but only a district of the Jaguarari municipality in Bahia, northeastern Brazil. Apart from the ubiquitous goats strolling its streets, everything else in Pilar looks disturbingly incongruent.

After driving through 110 kilometers of barren landscape from the nearest big town, Juazeiro, you arrive at an impeccably clean village of 8,000 inhabitants. Many of the buildings are three and four stories high, set along and among avenues and squares the size of soccer stadiums.

While there is obviously no shortage of space, engineers working for the copper mining company Mineração Caraíba indulged themselves by building modernist box-shaped houses planted on pillars that land right on the side of the road. The result is a kind of colonnade, with every sidewalk partially shaded by the first floor – a reasonable design, after all, in a landscape where the sun blazes for at least eight months of the year with virtually no rain, and the remaining four months bring, on average, just 440 millimeters of rainfall. Some years there is virtually none.

Pilar was built from nothing 35 years ago when the copper mine was commissioned. The company's strict hierarchy can still be seen in the house façades: one window for workers, two for the next in rank, three for group leaders, four for supervisors, and handsome bungalows for the engineers.

It was all supposed to last a hundred years, but just one decade after investing US$58 million, the company discovered that the copper ore in the open pit would run out long before that. Even though a new and deeper vein has been found and an underground mine started, the current projected shutdown date for the mine is 2007 or 2008. Not a ghost town, then; just one that has reached the zombie stage. And yet, this is a village that refuses to die as scheduled – and all because of its goats. Those hardy creatures patrolling its avenues are proving a desperately needed escape route.

Previous page: **For the sertanejos-the people of the Caatinga, Brazil's vast, arid biome-raising goats are good insurance against the worst of the dry times.**

Above: **Pilar village, built to house local copper miners, is a sprawling modernist anomaly in this wild region.**

Lost leaves, dry rivers

Pilar is set in the midst of probably the least known among Brazil's great biomes: the Caatinga. This huge tract of nearly 737,000 square kilometers sits in the driest portion of northeastern Brazil. The word *caatinga* comes from the indigenous Brazilian language Tupi, and means 'white forest' – a reference to the remarkable absence of green there during most of the year. The Caatinga's unique community of plants has evolved to drop all their leaves and retain what little humidity is left in their stems. In this semi-arid climate, where rivers can disappear in a matter of weeks, it's a useful adaptation.

Maria do Remédio Leite de Santana was born in Piauí, one of the poorest states in Brazil, which sits within the Caatinga. When her father, a cowboy, lost his sight in one eye, the family moved to a big city, Petrolina. This was Remédio's chance to keep studying. A zoo technician by training, she then ended up in Pilar, when her husband was hired to work for Mineração Caraíba, in the underground mine.

Not content to stay at home, she soon found herself engaged in social work for the mining company, and was given a daunting task: to help the people of Pilar find an economic alternative to save their village, and retain their regionally unheard-of amenities, such as paved roads and piped water (pumped from the São Francisco river through a pipeline 86 kilometers long). Managers at Mineração Caraíba have come up with a term to describe the project: 'perennialization.' It's a word that is also applied to what engineers try to do with the Caatinga rivers, which regularly evaporate into thin air.

Nature is not easily amenable, and a town's economic life may not be saved by dry logic. It is something of a paradox that Remédio is employed to help Pilar by a company that has laid off 1,000 of its staff over the last decade, and now threatens the villagers' livelihoods by going out of business. Moreover, the work has been a distinctly bumpy ride.

Remédio and her team tried varied approaches, such as training 300 of the village women as dressmakers. But it soon became clear that an artificial cottage industry alone would not

Above: **White forest: a unique community of plants erupt from the pale, flowing grasses of the Caatinga.**

be sufficient, in spite of more than 9 million hours of training, paid for by Caraíba. The company has, in fact, poured more than US$2 million of investment into the project over the past decade.

And it has done even more. In 1994 it transferred all real estate in the village to its employees, giving them a powerful incentive to remain there. To the people of Brazil's northeastern dry lands, that usually means a few dozen goats grazing in the Caatinga. A one-windowed house, by comparison, was wealth indeed.

Generations of these *sertanejos* have raised goats in this way as a kind of insurance against the worst dry seasons. (These tend to correlate with El Niño years, when unusual temperatures in surface waters of the Pacific off Peru disrupt weather patterns over all of South America.) Remédio and her husband themselves raise some 200 goats in their spare time.

As the rest of the production plans for the village were successively discarded, the goat raisers among the villagers began to realize they had the higher stake in the future survival of Pilar. They felt attached to the land. And they saw that the most promising route of escape was to be found in their own culture, built up over centuries of tense negotiations with the Caatinga. "All roads pointed to the goat," recalls Remédio.

Choosing a road

The Caatinga can astonish someone used to Brazil's lusher landscapes. In August, driving through the outskirts of Pilar's copper mine, you see a mosaic of landscapes shaped by soil characteristics and local availability of water. Pineapple-like plants known as *macambiras*, with worrisome thorny red blades, spring up in the hundreds out of the ground. A hundred meters ahead, the terrain is dominated by an impenetrable wood of the *favela*, a medium-sized tree full of spikes.

A minute later you are in cactus country, facing huge concentrations of *xique-xique*, *facheiro* and *mandacaru*. Keep driving and soon the plants start to become subtly greener, giving way to higher and thicker trees full of leaves – a clear indication that water is available and houses will appear.

Up a ramp full of rocks, and the bushes turn a dark grey, leading the outsider to conclude – wrongly – that it has been burned by farmers. But again, this is only the plants' defence against extreme dryness. Even more astonishing are the long stretches of whitened, dessicated grasses undulating under the glaring sun. There is only one common thread running through this extraordinary botanical patchwork: goats (and occasionally sheep). Besides birds and scattered lizards, goats are the only animals to be seen.

Traditionally, the *sertanejo* use a communal grazing area system known as *fundo de pasto*. Groups of up to 40 or 50 families share an unfenced stretch of Caatinga where the animals feed before returning every evening to spend the night in barns. An estimated 20,000 families in Bahia alone rely on this type of commons for their livelihood. The state has the largest goat herd in Brazil – about 3.5 million animals – as well as 2.7 million sheep.

But despite the huge herds, traditional husbandry methods have been highly unproductive. "Goats raised men, not the other way round," says Remédio.

Rainfall comes to the Caatinga – if at all – between November and March. As the land turns green, the does and ewes go into oestrus; but under the *fundo de pasto* conditions, the kids and lambs are born and feed far into the drought period. Parasites and disease tended to kill off more than half of them. Those able to survive take up to a year and a half to reach commercial weight, something in the range of 25 kilograms – only to be sold for a mere US$20 to the *atravessadores*, roaming buyers who make profits as high as 80 per cent just from transporting the animals to the nearest slaughterhouse.

Bypassing bottlenecks

Spotting the bottlenecks in making a living out of goat and sheep raising in Pilar was easy. Fixing them was another thing entirely.

Below: **Horse's watermelons** (*Citrullus lanatus cv. citroides*).

Around 1995, not long after Caraíba called the first meetings of Pilar's goat raisers, groups of small farmers from as far as 300 kilometers away began attending. Two years later the villagers and fellow goat raisers from the region formed the Federation of Semi-Arid Associations and Entities (FAESA), which later gave birth to the Agro-Industrial Cooperative of the Semi-Arid (COGRISA).

It was evident to both groups that productivity needed boosting, so they sought the technical support of two research facilities: the regional branch of the Brazilian Agricultural Research Corporation (EMBRAPA) and its state-level equivalent, the Agricultural Development Corporation of Bahia (EBDA).

While a long list of modern husbandry techniques has been introduced in the region since then, there has been resistance. Some traditionalists would not allow technicians to count the animals, as this was supposed to bring bad luck. Some refused even to hear of synchronizing the oestrus periods of does or ewes, saying that there was no need as oestrus would come naturally with the rain.

But while change has been slow, the villagers have been won over by a powerful demonstration of how the new techniques, such as a controlled mating season and the use of silos, can potentially free them from their heaviest burden – living at the whim of the region's climate.

Forage was always the biggest limiting factor. For at least six months of the year, the Caatinga cannot offer much to the animals, and they lose weight at a dramatic pace. To fill the gap, EMBRAPA developed the so-called CBL ('Caatinga, buffel grass, leucaena') system, for potential use in up to 400,000 square kilometers of the Caatinga.

CBL is a sustainable feeding system where natural pastures are complemented by two exotic plants: buffel grass (*Cenchrus ciliaris*), which is very resistant to drought and easily made into hay, and the leguminous *Leucaena leucocephala*.

Other forage plants can also be cultivated and added to the feeding mixture. Besides *palma* (the local name for the prickly pear, *Opuntia ficus indica*), another exotic plant introduced in Brazil's northeast a century ago, farmers also use *melancia-de-*

cavalo (horse's watermelon, *Citrullus lanatus cv. citroides*), that lasts up to two years on the ground where it has grown and has a 12 percent protein content. The plants are harvested continuously during the rainy season, chopped up in communal machines and either fed directly to the animals, or fermented in trench-silos 5 meters long and a meter deep. Fermented forage can keep for two years.

COGRISA has now grown to include around 2,500 farmer families who own some 145,000 goats and sheep. Since the introduction of exotic races bred for meat, such as Boer goats from South Africa, the kids are born weighing a healthy 4 or 5 kilograms. The animals reach commercial weight fast, in as few as 6 months. Parasite infestation is kept below 18 percent – a massive contrast with the 100 percent rates common a decade ago.

Slaughterhouse dreams

Now that they have seen the potential, Pilar's goat raisers want more. Nothing less than a slaughterhouse will suffice, complete with a meat-processing plant and tannery. As they see it, it is their only chance to appropriate the income ordinarily diverted elsewhere by the *atravessadores*.

The price tag for constructing and equipping such a complex is estimated at US$2.1 million. But it is an investment Bahia has been postponing for years. The members of COGRISA felt betrayed when a meat-processing plant was built in Juazeiro instead. "Our life project was the plant," says Remédio, who had put almost all her eggs in the state government's basket.

With or without a local plant, however, life has altered for the better around Pilar and the dying copper mine. Less than 15 kilometers away, the farm Lagoa do Caldeirão, owned by the Morgado family, is a case in point. The 72-year-old patriarch Manoel Ferreira Morgado is slowly transferring the reins to the youngest of his 8 children. This son, Paulo Roberto Rodrigues Morgado, has made big changes on the farm in just a year.

Below: **Weigh to go: by enhancing forage sustainably, goat raisers have seen kids reaching commercial weight in as little as half a year.**

A machine operator at Caraíba for the last 9 years, the younger Morgado daily covers the distance from his two-window home in Pilar to the farm by motorbike, the vehicle of choice in the region after donkeys went out of fashion.

The 1,000-hectare property is home to some 500 hens and a herd of 450 goats and sheep, besides 55 cows ("my father's obsession"). All are fed on a *fundo de pasto* the size of the farm, shared with 50 families, and a 10-hectare patch where he grows corn, *melancia-de-cavalo* and *palma*, among other forage plants. The family has bought no feed for three years now.

Income generated by the farm is admittedly low – just US$210 a month. "But it has the potential to yield 5,000 reais [about US$2,100] a month," dreams Morgado.

His dreams would be decidedly out of place in a novel of the magic realism school, though, simply because they are coming true. At least, he does not have to take the herd some 12 kilometers down the road to find water, as his father used to do when he was his age.

And Morgado has other plans for himself, once the mine closes shop: he wants to study veterinary medicine, and plans to pay the fees with money generated by his herd of top-class goats.

Above: **Local hero: the humble goat ensures Pilar will have an economic lifeline once the copper runs out.**

Marcelo Leite is a science writer in São Paulo, Brazil. The author of many books on biotechnology and environment themes, he writes a weekly science column for the daily Folha de S. Paulo.

Should mountain communities be paid to conserve their natural resources? Yes, according to a scheme from Mexico's cloud forests.

Moving mountains in Mexico

by Ehsan Masood

Previous page: **Wild west: West-central Mexico enjoys an abundance of biological diversity. The Sierra de Manantlán Biosphere Reserve is home to 2,700 plants species, 560 species of wildlife and one-third of the country's native birds.**

Right: **Cloud forests in the Sierra Madre.**

The four-by-four vehicle took a sharp turn and we found ourselves negotiating an unsurfaced track. I am with a small group of trainee environmental leaders preparing to spend two days in the heart of the 140,000-hectare Sierra de Manantlán Biosphere Reserve, a protected area that straddles the states of Jalisco and Colima in West-Central Mexico.

The reserve is a sort of mini-heaven for ecology, and hence a prime candidate for ecotourism. Established by the University of Guadalajara's Manantlán Institute of Ecology in 1986, it contains fir, pine, and oak forests, 2,700 other species of plants, 560 species of wildlife, and a third of Mexico's native birds. But this wasn't what was drawing my attention. Sprawling at the side of that dirt track was another world – of tin roofs, open fires, unrelenting cold and barefoot children.

Poverty and mountains ought to be poles apart. Mountains, after all, help to generate around wealth from tourism. But despite this, some 80 percent of all mountain-dwellers – approximately 10 percent of the world's population – live below the poverty line. The Sierra de Manantlán Biosphere Reserve is not much different. An estimated 30,000 people live within or off the land. The majority have little or no access to life's most basic needs – employment, healthcare, education. Incidences of infant mortality and infectious diseases are particularly high.

Nor, indeed, do they have much access to water. We are standing in the forest near what is called a karst, a large area inside the forest comprising mostly limestone rock. Enrique Jardel of the University of Guadalajara, who is with us, explains that when it rains, the water seeps straight through the karst and into the ground, feeding the three aquifers that supply the city of Colima immediately below the forest. For the people of the biosphere, it means that there are no flowing rivers and streams to draw water from. The best they can do is to collect water in buckets and tubs left outside during the rainy season. This water then has to be used during the seven months when there is no rain. During all this time, there is no purification, no drainage and no sanitation.

Greenbacks

Poverty is scant reward for a people whose frugal lifestyle keeps forests – and city water supplies – intact. And that is why a group comprising the University of Guadalajara, the federal government and local leaders have been backing a plan designed to get water and other basic services into the reserve itself.

The idea at the heart of the plan is a simple one. The people of Sierra de Manantlán should be compensated for living a lifestyle that helps to maintain both the reserve and what are called 'environmental services' that the reserve provides. These services include the absorbing of greenhouse gases by the forests, which helps to combat climate change; conserving species of plants and animals; protecting Colima City's water supplies; stopping soil erosion and protecting scenic beauty.

The idea that people should start paying for the services

that nature provides for free is controversial, but not at all new. Compensating people for environmental services has already been tested. In fact, it is well known in the field of environmental economics and was put into practice in 1996, in a new forestry law in Costa Rica.

Sergio Graf, an adviser to Mexico's National Water Commission, is one of the plan's architects. A Fellow of the non-profit Leadership for Environment and Development (LEAD), he was director of the Sierra de Manantlán Biosphere Reserve for its first nine years, until 2002.

Man with a plan

When he was first appointed to the post, the forest's community leaders were sceptical. They feared that they would lose their livelihoods if the land around their homes became part of what was effectively becoming a protected area. But in time they grew to trust him. Graf has helped to resolve many of their internal conflicts, so when he promised that conservation can benefit people as much as wildlife, the locals backed his work. Some even let their children train in conservation under him. And his successor as the reserve's director is a local son, and not someone parachuted in from another part of Mexico. Today, Graf has near-celebrity status and as we travel with him through the reserve, the reaction from local people is as if he were a Hollywood star stepping out onto the sidewalks of London or New York.

We arrive at a small clearing, where a group of Manantlán men and women are preparing a meal of barbecued meat, beans, and large tortilla-style bread being baked in what looks like a clay oven. We eat quickly as sunset isn't far off, after which the forest will descend into darkness until sunrise.

Graf says that the logic behind the idea of compensation for environmental services is something of a no-brainer. The reserve's communities need to develop, he says. They need to get out of poverty. They need housing, schools, jobs and healthcare, all of which costs money. However, the creation of the reserve has meant that they are not allowed to engage in logging, kill wildlife, or use water for irrigation in what are called 'core zones' in the forest.

Elsewhere in the forest, there are no objections and they could in theory cut down more trees, light more fires, or convert more land to cattle grazing. However, these actions would almost certainly have destabilizing consequences in the long term. The most obvious consequence from a degraded forest would be a reduction in the water that passes through the forest and supplies the city of Colima below.

Meeting of minds

So what form should compensation take? And who should foot the bill? This is where the plan gets controversial. Earlier, Graf has arranged for the group to attend a meeting of what is called

Above: **Military macaw.**

the Colima river basin council, where the plan would be unveiled. The council is broad-based and includes representatives from state and federal government, municipal authorities, universities and nongovernmental organizations, as well as the director of the reserve and leaders of Sierra de Manantlán's various communities.

At the meeting, we listen intently as Graf presents the plan, suggesting that compensation should take the form of a small tax on water charges paid by residents of Colima City. Most of the council members nod in agreement. One of Sierra de Manantlán's community leaders says: "This is important to us. We protect the forest, and we need support for doing this." The representative of Mexico's federal environment ministry chimes in, saying: "If we don't pay now, the cost of cleaning up and the environmental consequences will be much higher."

But the meeting is far from plain sailing. Opposition comes from an important quarter. One delegate representing Colima City's municipal authority says that collecting existing water charges is difficult in itself. An additional tax, while attractive in theory, would be unworkable in practice. Another delegate from Colima City suggests that industry, rather than domestic consumers, should compensate the reserve's inhabitants. "We have no money to pay. We don't even have money to trace the leaks from which we lose 30 per cent of our city's water supply. Ecology may be important for the future, but people will not want to pay anything now."

The full extent of the opposition becomes clearer later that evening, however, when we are invited to a meeting hosted by the Colima state government. One government official says it appears to him that the reserve's inhabitants want to be compensated for something that if fact does not belong to them. "It is important that the state helps small communities get access to fresh water," he says. "But water that passes through a community does not automatically belong to that community; it is the property of the nation."

Graf and his colleagues recognize that they have much work to do. But they are used to steering their way out of setbacks, and are confident of eventual success. The bottom line, he says, is that conservation will never work without social development; and the quicker the authorities realize this and put it into practice, the better it will be for all.

University for the poor

The creation of the Sierra de Manantlán Biosphere Reserve was prompted by the discovery in 1979 of a wild relative of corn, known as *Zea diploperennis*. This attracted international attention because of its potential in improving what is the world's second most important cereal. A small research office, known as the Las Joyas Research Station, was established by the University of Guadalajara and the Jalisco state government to protect the corn's habitat.

The research station has since grown into the Manantlán Institute of Ecology. Today, the institute is better known as a voice for those who live in the reserve, and helps to articulate their concerns to those in authority, says Eduardo Santana, the director of the institute. In that respect, it is a fairly unique institution in that it has made the leap from being an observer, and is now a participant, activist and lobbyist on behalf of some of Mexico's poorest people.

Initially, the institute's work among local people focused on creating awareness of the biosphere reserve's existence, as well as general environmental education programs. But Santana says that he and his colleagues soon discovered that the reserve's communities had a range of unmet social needs, such as education, healthcare, housing and jobs. The institute brought in local people to participate in its research work.

The institute also became involved in a struggle between local indigenous communities and private logging companies over control of land and forests. The forest land is communally owned by local people under what is called the *Ejido* system. However, much of this has been lost to illegal logging. When the University of Guadalajara proposed setting up a biosphere reserve in the forest, many local communities saw this as a first step in protecting their land from unwanted logging.

Ehsan Masood writes on science and technology in developing countries, and is based in London.

The Inca revered the vicuña. Now
their ancient traditions are being
revived to protect this shy Andean
animal while bringing local people
real financial reward.

Going for gold in the Andes

by Fred Pearce

They call it the camel of the Americas and the queen of the high Andes. In the days of the Inca, the vicuña was a sacred beast. Anyone who killed one of these shy mammals without permission would themselves be slaughtered. Their wool – the finest and warmest in the world – was the preserve of monarchs.

Then came the Europeans. From the Spanish conquistadors to the British trading companies of the 20th century, their lust for the wool of the vicuña almost brought about its extinction. But now, with an irony the Inca would have appreciated, the animal's most prized asset – its exquisite wool – is coming to its rescue. Conservationists, governments and the peasant people of the Andes are all beginning to realize that returning to ancient Incan methods is the key to the vicuña's future.

Woolly wonder

Previous page: **'Queen of the Andes' and an object of veneration to ancient monarchs, the vicuña is now heralded as a saviour of altiplano economies and a conservation success story.**

Above: **This smallest of the South American camelids yields a fine golden wool – the most valuable commodity in the high Andes.**

The wool of the vicuña is the most valuable commodity in the high Andean plains. So says Don Nicolas Maidana, a farmer in Cieneguillas, an *altiplano* village of 200 people in Jujuy, the most northwesterly province in Argentina, which borders both Chile and Bolivia. The local herd of some 900 vicuña used to be a pest here, he says. They tore down fences, gnawed at the pastures and brought disease to local flocks of llamas. But now, he says, "they are an important resource for us. Once we started capturing and shearing them, we can see an economic return".

He is not alone. In 2003, Maidana and dozens of his fellow farmers in these wild mountain lands joined in a roundup of vicuña in Argentina. As conservation scientists from Chile, Argentina and Britain looked on, more than 100 people from the poor llama-herding villages of Jujuy walked across the hills waving coats and colored flags as they gently persuaded dozens of vicuña – each elegant, long-necked beast as high as a person's chest – to walk into a wire and canvas stockade for shearing.

There was a good deal of enthusiasm. This was a money-making day after all. Each animal yielded around 250 grams of fine, golden wool. Once cleaned and woven, it fetched grams of fine, golden wool. Once cleaned and woven, it fetched up to US$100 in European markets – and some probably ended up in coats for sale in Milan stores at up to 25,000 Euro each. "Wildlife has become our ally and not our enemy," says Maidana.

The Andean highlands of Peru, Bolivia, northern Chile and Argentina are a tough, unforgiving environment of thin air, cold temperatures, poor soils and tough grass, surrounded by snow-capped mountains. Human population densities today are low – much lower than in the days of the Inca, whose great civilization is the only one ever to have truly mastered this land.

One of the Inca's masterful techniques was the harvesting of wool from the great herds of wild vicuña that once roamed the highlands. The vicuña climb to 5,000 meters using adapted red blood cells that boost their absorption of oxygen in the thin air, special teeth for chewing the tough local grasses and thick, ultra-fine hair to survive the cold.

The Inca banned the hunting of vicuñas, which had

Below: **High plains drifters: a roving band of vicuña 'bachelors' graze a sere hillside.**

probably been going on in the Andes for at least 10,000 years before their empire was established. But the wool was too precious to pass up, so they devised a harvesting technique called the *chaku*. During this vast communal activity, tens of thousands of people would spill out across the hillsides, forming human chains to round up and corral thousands of vicuña. Shepherded into enclosures, the vicuña would be sheared of their wool, then released back into the wild.

Every one of the millions of vicuña living here could expected to be shorn every two or three years. It was an exquisite exercise in what is today called sustainable management.

End of a world

When spun, vicuña wool produces a light, beautiful cloth. The cloth was the ultimate symbol of power in the Inca world. Legend has it that only the emperor could put on a new coat made of the vicuña's wool. He would wear it once – then pass it on to relatives or courtiers in return for offerings to the gods. The *chaku* and its harvest was thus a system of social control as well as of resource management.

All this ended with the arrival of the Spanish conquistadors about 500 years ago. With them came the collapse of Incan civilization. The *chaku*, while never entirely eliminated, lost its place in the society and ecology of the *altiplano*. The conquistadors hunted the vicuña with firearms, killing the animals for meat as well as its wool, which they exported to Spain.

This was no sustainable harvest; it was another Wild West. Within a decade Spanish chroniclers were recording a decline in vicuña numbers. In the late 18th century, as many as 50,000 vicuña were being slaughtered annually. This prompted the first, albeit ineffectual, European-style conservation laws to protect vicuña, which were passed in 1777 by the Spanish imperial court.

The trade went on, however, with growing involvement by the state and later by modern European firms, principally

Opposite: **Shear beauty: the chaku, a ceremony during which vicuña are sheared and released, is a classic of sustainable management.**

from Britain. By the late 1960s, as European markets grew, vicuñas were close to what population biologists have called "year zero." There were fewer than 10,000 individuals still roaming the *altiplano*, waiting to be hunted down by poaching gangs.

In the nick of time, emergency legislation passed under international rules banned all hunting or capture of vicuña, and shut down the trade in their wool. In 1979 the vicuña got its own treaty, signed by Argentina, Peru, Bolivia and Chile and many of its core habitats became protected areas. Numbers began to recover, and there have been spectacular increases across the *altiplano* – but now that progress is under threat again, say conservationists.

Weaving a strategy

The vicuña is the smallest of the four members of the camelid family in South America. The others are the guanaco, their wild lowland cousin, and the llama and alpaca, both of which have long since been domesticated. Recent genetic studies suggest that thousands of years ago the alpaca was bred from the vicuña, and the llama from the guanaco.

Vicuñas form family groups with a male, his harem and their young. These groups are highly territorial. For 30 years now they have been protected by armed guards patrolling the protected areas where most lived, keeping out poachers. The females produce only one cria, or offspring, a year. But with many predators like the Andean fox in decline, survival rates were good and populations soared – so high in places that shepherds and farmers complained that the animals were invading their pastures.

There may be as many as 250,000 vicuña in the *altiplano* today. More than half are in Peru, but several thousand have crossed the border into Ecuador, where they were previously extinct. In Peru's biggest protected area, the Pampas Galeras reserve in the arid south of the country, densities rose as high as 30 vicuña per square kilometer.

In places, they are now perceived as protected pests. The

armed patrols set up to protect the animals have sometime spent more time carrying out culls than warding off hunters. In Pampa Galeras, there was controversy when it emerged that local officials at the international environmental organization World Wildlife Fund persuaded the WWF office in Europe to fund the purchase of guns and ammunition for a cull that took place in late 1979 and which may have killed 10,000 animals and spawned an illicit trade in frozen vicuña meat.

Conservation scientists and governments of the vicuña homelands decided that the best way to prevent a breakdown of the conservation strategy was to allow peasants to make money out of living vicuña. "We decided to bring back the ancient *chaku* technique from the Incan empire. This gave a chance for poor local communities, which often earn less than US$500 a year, to benefit from the golden fleece," says Cristián Bonacic. An Oxford University-trained veterinarian, Bonacic has been working on protecting the vicuña and their lowland cousin the guanacos for 20 years. He created his own conservation group, Fauna Australis, in Chile in 2001.

In many places, park guards have handed control of the vicuña to local communities, teaching them how to round up the animals for shearing. The first handovers began around the Pampa Galeras reserve. There, says British academic Jerry Laker of the Macaulay Institute in Aberdeen, Scotland, villages like Lucanas near Nazca now make their living largely from wild vicuña.

The international community has responded. Exports of vicuña wool were allowed again in 1995. And now the approach is extending to other countries in the Andes. European conservationists have weighed in with a project called Manejo de Camélidos Silvestres (MACS), which aims to improve the sustainability of the *chaku*.

A weaving mill opened in Peru's second city, Arequipa, to handle the growing amounts of wool awaiting export – the only manufacturing plant in the world to do so. Its production is around 2 tons of wool a year. And the product is in great demand. At around a hundredth of a millimeter thick, the vicuña wool fibers are finer and lighter than their much-touted rivals cashmere, mohair, angora and shahtoosh.

Return of the *chaku*

The *chaku* has become a weekend tourist attraction across Peru. But it remains, as in the time of the Inca, a mostly part-time activity carried out by whole communities and with fair shares for all in the proceeds. Like the Inca emperors, the conservation scientists behind the plan see it as an exercise in social cohesion. And the Quechua people of Peru are reviving the half-remembered ancient ceremonies that accompanied the *chaku*. As the animals are corralled, an "Inca king" blesses the ceremony and takes blood from behind the ears of the two best animals before shearing begins – just as they did 500 years ago.

"As an example of live harvesting of wildlife products, it is probably unique," says Laker, who is project leader for MACS. Some communities make US$250,000 a year from their part-time *chaku*s. But bickering over who gets the spoils sometimes seems to have hampered enthusiasm for regular roundups, even among the poor communities of the *altiplano*. For many, the idea of a communal activity to harvest wool from a wild animal is, in the modern world of privatized resources and profits, a hard one to countenance.

So things may be moving on. The commercial success of the *chaku* is actually encouraging methods of intensifying and privatizing the wool harvest. By degrees, the vicuña is being turned into a farm animal. In Chile they are breeding vicuña in captivity. And here and there in Argentina, the animals are being captured and domesticated on vicuña farms. There is a half-way house too. In Peru, they are trying out the farming of half-wild vicuña on large ranches of up to 10,000 hectares.

There are growing fears about the effect of this process of gradual domestication on the animals. Comparisons are being made with the farm-based 'harvesting' of other wildlife products – like draining bile from the Chinese moon bear, or musk from deer – practices which have become bywords for cruelty. "There are serious animal welfare concerns," says Bonacic. "In a captive situation, the animals become chronically stressed."

A big concern of conservationists is that the international laws that allow trading vicuña wool make no distinction between

Previous page: **Communal commerce: Every stage (clockwise from far right) – shearing, gathering up the wool, taking down the fences and final release of the animals back into the wild- the chaku is an activity involving entire communities. For some, it means profits of up to US$250,000 a year.**

wool from wild and domesticated animals on vicuña farms –
even though the conservation implications of the two approaches
are vastly different.

"Captive breeding is not the way to conserve the
species," says Bonacic. In fact, he fears it could be the death of
the species in the wild, because it undermines the incentives for
conservation of the animals on the *altiplano*. Right now, villagers
want to protect the wild herds because they are the only source of
the "golden fleece," he says. "But if I can keep a vicuña in a
corral for my own benefit, feed the animal with alfalfa and take
care of the herd as I would a llama herd, why should I conserve
the vicuña in the wild?"

"We are already seeing an increase in poaching, and the
lack of distinction between captivity and wild harvest is one
cause," says Bonacic "It is threatening what has been a very
successful conservation program, but nobody seems to recognize
this." The risk, he says, is ultimately that the entire species could
be turned into a farm animal, like the llama and alpaca before it.
And it could happen under the banner of the 'sustainable
harvest' of wild animals.

One day, South America may wake up to find it has
plenty of vicuñas – but none of them wild. It may be a thousand
years old, but the Inca *chaku* seems to be the only way forward.

*Fred Pearce is Environment
Consultant to* New Scientist
magazine and is based in London.

Saving Egypt's songbird

by Nadia El-Awady

Bird trapping is big on the Sinai peninsula – but thanks to grassroots conservation, one threatened species is getting through the net.

Previous page: **Zaranik, a marshy protected area on the Sinai Peninsula, lies directly under one of the corncrake's autumn migratory routes.**

Above: **Hunted on Egypt's northern coast and with its habitat threatened by European monoculture, the corncrake (*Crex crex*) is now recognized as globally vulnerable.**

As the autumn sun rises on the northern shores of the Sinai peninsula, a cool breeze blows in from the Mediterranean. With it comes a flock of corncrakes, just arriving on their long journey from the shores of southern Europe. The birds land, exhausted by the 10-hour non-stop flight over the sea, and scuttle under the dry shrubs that cover the area.

This is just a brief stop for the birds en route to their wintering grounds in sub-Saharan Africa. Shattered by the first leg of the trip, they are completely unaware of the local trappers following their footprints in the dew-moistened sands. All the hunters need to do to catch their bird is fling a small net over the shrub where it's hiding.

The corncrake (*Crex crex*) is considered an easy catch and a cheap source of meat by the people of Egypt's northern coast. But the Sinai peninsula – where so much of the hunting takes place – is becoming a much safer place for this shy bird. For over a decade, international conservationists, Egypt's government agencies and the local people have been involved in a cooperative effort to save it from further threat.

Safe haven

The Sinai Peninsula falls under one of the corncrake's four major migratory routes. And up to 30 percent of the birds flying over Egypt land in Zaranik, a 250-square-kilometer tract embracing the eastern end of Bardawil lake in northern Sinai.

Designated a protected area in 1985, Zaranik lives up to its name. Translated as 'meandering waterways,' the area encompasses a shallow, salty lagoon scattered with numerous densely vegetated islets. Its shores are fringed with mudflats and saltmarshes, and further inland, the man-made evaporation beds of a salt works that blend into the dune-covered landscape beyond.

In mid-August, waterbirds can be seen in the shallows to either side of Zaranik's makeshift dirt roads. It is hot, humid but fanned by that fresh sea breeze. The few registered fishers cast their nets into the glittering water as Egyptian border police vigilantly pace up and down, ensuring that only those with the right certification get into the reserve. Next month, in September, the corncrakes will arrive.

That many still do is largely due to a remarkable three-year project in the late-1990s. This was geared specifically to protecting the corncrake from hunting during its stopover in northern Sinai and part of Egypt's north coast. By then, the bird had already been recognized as vulnerable both globally and in Europe, listed in Appendix II of the 1979 Convention on the Conservation of European Wildlife and Natural Habitats and Appendix II of the Convention on the Conservation of Migratory Species.

Waheed Salama, Director-General of Egypt's Department of Protected Areas and one of two main researchers on the project, explains that the project's main goal had been promoting awareness among the people of Sinai on how to live sustainably with their surroundings. "Today, it's essential to involve local people in projects such as this," says Salama. "They are the most qualified to understand the problems we need to address, and to cooperate in finding solutions."

Zaranik's current director, Saad Othman, remembers the

Above: **East meets west: a Bedouin tending goats near Lake Bardawil in Zaranik tops her veil with a baseball cap.**

flurry of activity at the time of the project, when he had just arrived to work in the reserve. Othman originally studied agriculture and, as one of the top students of his class, seemed bound for an academic career. His mischievous personality, however, failed to fit the usual profile of university teachers, and he ended up going to Zaranik as an employee of the Egyptian Environmental Agency. Enthusiasm and a lively mind suit environmental protection work perfectly, and Othman felt himself at home.

Now in his mid-thirties, he speaks with a sparkle in his eye about the various projects he has been involved in at Zaranik. Educational outreach was hugely important from the start. "Our awareness program began with simply visiting schools, summer clubs, and libraries with our briefcases in hand," he says.

A second stage involved giving workshops to science teachers in the area. "This forged a link between the local schools and their nearest protected area," he explains.

Greening the generations

Conservation awareness programs commonly focus on youth – who are, after all, potential hunters – and in 1996, Zaranik opened its gates to the first school and university field trips. It was a trickle that became a flood: a decade later, there are 100 such visits a year.

Just as essential to the project's aims was providing information and services to local people, many from Bedouin

Above: **Red dawn: before the conservation project at Zaranik took off, the migratory stopover at the east end of Zaranik was a virtual avian death trap.**

communities. The Bedouin here live as they have for centuries, in reed huts scattered along the shores of Bardawil lake. They raise some sheep: mothers and daughters can often be seen on the shore, watering the animals as the men get their fishing boats ready for the day's catch. But during the migratory season, many of these men turn hunter to enhance their day's earnings and fill the family pot with soup.

Discussions with the hunters was a major focus of the project. When it was suggested that they stop hunting the corncrake for a few years, local elders noted that, in fact, the numbers of corncrakes coming to Egypt had decreased over the past years. Project workers explained that if the corncrakes were left alone for some time, their numbers would rise once more, allowing for sustainable hunting in the future.

Trappers were also given guidelines on how to hunt more sustainably. They were urged, for instance, to release corncrakes that had been accidentally snared by the nets used to catch quail (a delicacy in Egypt). The quail nets themselves were also subject to new restrictions. These had to be 2 meters high or less to allow corncrakes – which fly higher than quail – a better chance of missing them. For the same reason, they had to be placed 500 meters or more inland. To allow escape routes for the corncrakes, the nets had to have 25 meters' worth of gaps for every 100 meters of netting. Finally, no hunting whatsoever was to be allowed in Zaranik.

But it wasn't just trapping that threatened corncrakes in Sinai. Overgrazing and harvesting the brush for wood were also threatening the birds' habitat. To redress the balance, livestock owners were taught better methods of feeding their animals. They were provided with loans allowing them to buy a special brew of animal feed developed by Egyptian agriculturalists that would make their animals healthier. Some 40,000 acacia saplings were given to local communities to be planted and eventually used for sustainable grazing and wood collection. And handicrafts were taught to the local communities as an alternative livelihood to trapping.

"When people see all this, they feel the protected area is with them and not against them," says Othman. This, he affirms, has encouraged local communities to become involved in conservation activities at Zaranik long after the project itself ended.

Conservation in action

During the early days, when the project itself was running, such activities could be surprisingly lively. Mohamed Hassan, a guard at Zaranik, fondly remembers how scientists would sometimes take matters into their own hands. Hassan worked closely with Andrew Grieve of the UK-based Ornithological Society of the Middle East, Caucasus and Central Asia, who, with Salama, made up the senior research team.

"Andrew was at war," chuckles Hassan. He explains that whenever Grieve found illegitimate hunting activities going on in Zaranik, he would tear the nets apart with his bare hands. There is reason to be cautiously optimistic about the combined effect of such local efforts. In 2004, the corncrake was categorized as "nearly threatened" in the World Conservation Union (IUCN) Red List of threatened species, marginally down from its "threatened" status of 1988. This may seem a modest upturn in status, but it is still good news.

Recent estimates show that numbers worldwide have risen significantly. Marco Barbieri, the scientific and technical officer of the Secretariat of the UN Convention on Migratory Species, says there could be a number of reasons for this – but that the data needs careful interpretation.

"On one side, there has been conservation action that is likely to have had some results on the ground – and this has resulted locally in conservation of the species," says Barbieri. "At the same time, only a few years ago it was thought that the total number of birds in its migratory range was in the few hundreds of thousands." So some caution is advised in picking apart the evidence.

Says Barbieri, "The species is not necessarily recovering. It is likely some have. But many birds have not been counted before. It is information on the species that has improved in recent years." Barbieri says the most recent estimates for the global population of corncrakes indicate that there are anywhere from around 1.5 million to 3.5 million singing males (that is, males of reproductive age). "That means you might have up to 6 million adult birds," he says.

So there is reason to be cheerful about the fate of the corncrake, for now. Most realize that as conservation work makes that optimism possible, it has got to go on. The ongoing field trips and educational outreach at Zaranik are an important component, but even more vital is the work in Europe.

"A few years ago, [hunting in Egypt] was thought to have a significant impact," says Barbieri. "The fact is that at the moment, this is not one of the main threats to the species. Instead, it is the loss of habitat in the [corncrake's] reproductive areas in Europe and Asia." This was also the conclusion of the Zaranik project.

Corncrakes are reclusive birds that spend most of their time hiding in tall vegetation, so hayfields are an ideal habitat. Now, however, mechanized mowing and changing from traditional hay cutting to silage production are causing high chick mortality rates. An increase in sheep grazing has also reduced nesting habitats, as the animals strip tall grasses and other vegetation from the land.

Meanwhile, the use of herbicide and chemical fertilizers is reducing the variety of weeds and other vegetation that harbor insects – the mainstay of the birds' diet.

Europe now has a range of measures in place. Conservation action plans there include encouraging farmers to mow their lands in the summer months to give the corncrake chicks a better chance of reaching adulthood. Mowing practices have also been changed to begin in the middle of the field and circle outward, giving the birds a chance to scamper away through the yet uncut sections of the field.

Our interdependence with nature can, at times, turn into an ugly struggle. Yet as the quiet revolution at Zaranik shows, a balance can be struck. People can discover new, sustainable livelihood. And the corncrake – which many at Sinai once viewed as a mere morsel for the pot – can be promised safe landings.

Opposite: **Lake Bardawil, Zaranik.**

Glimpsing an avian recluse

Crex crex, the corncrake's scientific name, is an approximation of the bird's unusual rasping call.

The bird is larger than the quail and often mistaken for one. Corncrake is sold on the market in Egypt. With less meat than a quail, it costs 3LE (about 50 American cents) per pair, compared to 7LE (about US$1.20) per pair of quail.

The corncrake's breeding grounds extend over much of northern and central Europe and eastwards to Russia and central Siberia. The bird arrives at its breeding grounds starting from mid-April, and remains there until mid-August. Afterwards it begins its long journey south, crossing the Mediterranean along four major migratory routes. It rests along the southern shores for a day, before continuing its journey south to its wintering grounds in sub-Saharan Africa.

Corncrakes hide in meadows, marshlands and bushy forest clearings. Their reclusive habits mean that population numbers are difficult to pin down.

The birds breed from their first year of life with the males calling to attract females. Once they have mated, the male moves some distance away and begins to sing to attract a second mate.

Females build the nests on the ground, hidden by tall vegetation. The eggs take about 16 to 19 days to hatch. The mother feeds her chicks for about 10 to 15 days. Corncrakes feed mostly on insects, and to a lesser extent on vegetation and seeds.

Along with its listed status in various conventions, the corncrake is included in the African-Eurasian Waterbird Agreement (AEWA), which entered into force on November 1 1999. AEWA is the largest agreement of its kind developed so far under the UN Convention on the Conservation of Migratory Species, involving 51 countries in Europe, Asia, the Middle East and Africa, and Canada. An action plan for its conservation was produced in 2000 under the Convention on the Conservation of Migratory Species.

Nadia El-Awady is Health and Science Editor at the Web portal IslamOnline.Net, which is based in Cairo.

Reclaiming Jordan's Badia

by John Bohannon

What brings depleted drylands springing back to life? In Jordan's Badia desert, it is all down to mixing Bedouin know-how with cutting-edge science.

Previous page: **The seemingly dead, boulder-strewn flats of the Badia in Jordan's arid north pulse with life if you know where to look.**

Above: ***Pseudotrapelus sinaitus*, a reptile of the Badia.**

The phrase 'lunar landscape' might have been invented for Jordan's arid northern region, the Badia. You could literally fry an egg on one of the black basalt boulders peppering the flats, a legacy of ancient volcanic action. Reddish dust drifts across a parched ground that receives little more than 200 millimeters of rain in a good year. Yet, a fragile web of life thrives here.

Hidden in every nook and cranny are seeds that wait sometimes years for a brief soaking. As soon as it comes, the Badia explodes with flowers and the rushed rituals of mating animals, squeezing everything it can out of the moisture before it evaporates.

Like the plants and animals, the Badia's Bedouin people tune their lives to a schedule set by water. To capture as much of the brief springtime rain as possible, they guide runoff water to central pits to reduce evaporation. Once the long, dry summer hits, they turn to what they call their *falaj*, spring-fed watering systems that use plastered pipes stretching for kilometers underground. All the while, they rely on the sparse rain-fed plants to feed their herds of goats and sheep.

The Bedouin way of life has been sustained in the Badia with the help of one of the world's earliest environmental regulations. The tribal code known as *al-Himma*, Arabic for protection, prevents herders from letting animals overgraze the communal pastures. Repeat offenders can have their livestock confiscated. Water resources are inherited like family jewels and used strictly on the basis of need, with drinking and sanitation the top priority.

This is how life went on in the Badia for millennia. But times have changed. Jordan's population has swollen fivefold over the past 50 years, concentrated mostly in cities like the capital, Amman. Better roads and communication with these urban areas have brought market forces to the Badia. Water has been pumped from its rain-charged aquifers to feed the growing cities. Meanwhile, a booming demand for red meat has made a scaling-up of animal herding inevitable. And as governments forced the Bedouin to abandon nomadism for the settled life, agriculture expanded without long-term management plans.

The results have been disastrous. Large herds of goats

Above: **A qaà, or shallow depression in the land, collects water in winter and leaves valuable sediments behind when it evaporates.**

and sheep were allowed to nibble plants right to the stem, preventing seed production. Using equipment and techniques more suited to a temperate climate, farmers depleted the soil in one area and moved on to the next. Intensive pumping for irrigation lowered the water table and increased the soil's salinity to the point where nothing could grow on it. The Badia's familiar wildlife began to disappear. By the early 1990s, wildfires raged frequently across a landscape of dead brush.

But that's when the Jordanians sprang into action to save the Badia from collapse. Their progress in balancing the needs of local people with the protection of natural resources is being held up as an example of how modern life can be sustained in arid environments.

Lay of the land

With the help of charitable organizations, the Jordan Badia Research and Development Centre (BRDC) was inaugurated in

Above: **Rich pickings: two men work in Badia fields irrigated by a groundwater aquifer.**

1995. Its focus area is the northeastern panhandle of the country, which represents 15 percent of the Badia.

Why the panhandle? Conditions there are some of the harshest in the country, so solutions in this strip of land should work everywhere else. The area also contains a large proportion of critical resources, including most of the endangered plant and animal species as well as the Azraq oasis, an important source of water for the whole region.

"We knew we couldn't resurrect the dead," says Mohammed Shahbaz, head of the BRDC, "so the first question was, what do we still have?" To answer that, the center embarked on a massive survey of the area, both of its people and the natural resources, with the help of the UK's Royal Geographical Society and the Centre for Overseas Research and Development at the University of Durham, UK.

The first step was the creation of a field research center,

which was housed in the buildings of a former oil-pumping station in Safawi, about 150 kilometers east of Amman. This became a headquarters for researchers as well as a central depot for the rivers of data that have rolled in.

The picture that emerged was of an environment undergoing rapid change. Birds that normally roosted in the Badia were avoiding it. Some animals that can be found nowhere else, such as species of fish, frogs, and snakes specially adapted to the Badia, were dangerously close to extinction. Most of those species are familiar only to the Bedouin, but others are iconic, such as the pugnacious blue-striped killifish that ekes out a life in the Badia's springfed pools.

The Bedouin themselves were also changing. Only 5 percent were still fully nomadic herders by the 1990s; the rest had settled permanently in villages. Large-scale farming was something new to them and they faced "a steep learning curve," says Shahbaz.

Not surprisingly, the biggest challenge was the limited water supply. Digging more wells to irrigate crops only hastened depletion of the resource. The survey revealed exactly where water shortages were showing up, and where they were likely to hit next. By 2000, the BRDC was ready to shift from gathering information to applying it to solutions.

Brain gain

"What no one wanted to see was the Bedouin becoming displaced from their land," recalls Shahbaz. This is what happened to the Bedouin of Syria after a catastrophic drought in the late 1950s. Once those tribes dissolved and assimilated into the cities, their way of life disappeared forever. "The only option is to involve them in the entire process, and that's just what we've done."

Far from being a challenge, including local people has proven to be the BRDC's greatest asset. First of all, "no one knows the land better than the Bedouin," says Shahbaz, but they are also becoming well-trained local scientific experts in their

Opposite: **A Pistachio atlantica tree grows near a pool in the Beqeaweyay region of northern Badia.**

homeland. Through an exchange program set up between the BRDC and collaborating universities abroad, 15 Bedouin have obtained masters and PhD degrees.

The typical outcome of such investments is brain drain. Resisting the promise of Western salaries is difficult. But amazingly, every one of the highly trained Bedouin has returned to apply their knowledge to the Badia. Shahbaz, for one, is not surprised. "They are fiercely proud of their culture and want to come back to make a difference," he says.

One of the success stories is Ra'ed Jazi Al-Tabini, who grew up in the Badia and earned a PhD in agricultural science from the University of Newcastle in the UK. Now deputy president of the BRDC, he focuses on optimizing grazing practices. "I am quite optimistic," says Al-Tabini, "because I see the difference I am making here. The situation is truly improving."

With familiar faces running it, the BRDC's ideas for improving the state of the Badia have been eagerly embraced by the Bedouin, says Shahbaz. "They are open to good ideas, and have many of their own, too."

Those ideas are very much needed. The crisis facing the Badia is complex, and has no easy solutions. But given the right knowledge, small efforts can go a very long way to help with many of the problems. Just choosing which crop to grow can mean the difference between a sustainable future for the land and its caretakers, or disaster for both.

Creative cultivation

"If you want to grow tomatoes, that requires 150 liters of water to produce a single kilogram of harvest," points out Shahbaz. In temperate regions, that equation makes sense, "but we are the most water-poor nation in the Middle East, so we have to make the most of what is here." Water-intensive crops like tomatoes and melons are grown by farmers in the Badia, but only because the seeds and know-how are readily available. So the BRDC has been working hard to provide alternatives to these crops.

Shahbaz is quick to add that Western scientists have not trotted into the Badia like knights in shining armor rescuing a helpless people. "The Bedouin have a wealth of indigenous knowledge, so it was always a matter of making the most of science and tradition." A prime example is the Badia's native wild almond tree.

You wouldn't want to bite into one of its nuts – trace amounts of cyanide make it horribly bitter and even dangerous in large doses. The almonds you buy at your grocery store come from domesticated versions of the tree. However, the species is perfectly adapted to the Badia's bone-dry conditions, so wild almond groves are being planted in parts of the area that have lost vegetation.

The tree also has another use. To give farmers a better option than tomatoes and melons, BRDC researchers turned to the ancient art of grafting, the botanical transplantation procedure that brought us the apple. In contrast to the animal

Above: **Goats are central to the Bedouin domestic economy, but as herds have swollen to satisfy the growing demand for meat, vegetation in the Badia has thinned disastrously.**

world, trees are often happy to accept a severed branch – even if it hails from a different species. By grafting part of a peach tree onto wild almond, Bedouins now have a crop that can survive temperatures of 49°C heat and needs just 50 millimeters of water a year.

Grassroots action

Animal husbandry is a vital part of Bedouin life, so the BRDC next turned its attention to sustainable herding. "There was no problem when the ratio between people and their animals was kept small and relatively constant," says Shahbaz – that is, a maximum of a few dozen sheep and goats per household. But numbers today approach 400 per household. Traditional grazing is impossible with this kind of population, so the animals have had to be fed with imported grain.

The BRDC is trying to close the loop by encouraging the cultivation of Sudan grass, a hardy forage crop that grows well in the Badia. Other interventions include helping the Bedouin develop ownership schemes that encourage long-term protection of grazing lands, rather than short-term exploitation. Instead of letting herders rent small patches of land for one-year stints, those patches are being consolidated into single properties owned either by the village or by individuals who agree to follow sustainable grazing.

Ten years on, there are signs that the BRDC's efforts are making a difference in the local environment. Researchers have worked hand-in-hand with the Bedouin to set aside and protect critical areas like the Azraq oasis. At the last count, over 160 bird species have returned to roost between migrations. Native species that were teetering on the brink are making a recovery – including the killifish, which is being helped by a breeding program. "The major challenge is just to let people know about the importance of these natural resources," says Shahbaz. To that end, the BRDC is building an environmental awareness centre that, he says, will be part museum and part zoo for educational outreach.

Some surprising avenues for a better future in the Badia have also sprouted up. The traditional Bedouin tent may become the basis for a tidy industry. They are woven from goat hair and are by far the most comfortable sleeping arrangement in the desert. Breathable during the day, they are well insulated at night – and rain-proof, if needed, as the hairs swell when wet. A single tent will go for US$2,700, and the BRDC is helping the Bedouin scale up their production. "We already have orders coming in from abroad," says Shahbaz.

But the tents are just one example of new industries in the Badia. The Jordanian government is eyeing up this vast, wind-swept region as a potential site for solar and wind farms. Hundreds of ruined palaces from the many civilizations that have called the Badia home over the millennia, not to mention the wildlife of the restored Azraq oasis, beckon to an as yet undeveloped tourism industry.

All of these possibilities should translate to sustainable jobs for local people. "As long as we manage it carefully and work together, that should take agricultural pressure off the land," says Shahbaz. "The Badia does have a future."

Above: **Dream weavers: Bedouin expertise in spinning and weaving goat wool rugs is poised to pay handsomely – a traditional wool tent currently fetches US$2,700.**

John Bohannon is a contributing correspondent for Science *magazine, and is based in Berlin*

The wisdom of Morocco's women

by Catherine Brahic

Women discovered agriculture. No surprises then that farming in the rural villages of Morocco is being shaped by their unique knowledge, skills, and experience.

Previous page: **The Atlas mountains of Morocco are home to some of the oldest communities in the Middle East and North Africa.**

Above: **Brain gain: Despite little or no formal schooling, the Chorfa women of the High Ziz valley have developed specialized knowledge of agriculture.**

They say women were the first farmers.

In the fertile crescent of Mesopotamia, some 6,000 or 7,000 thousand years before the birth of Jesus Christ, men spent most of their time hunting. The job of gathering wild cereals such as wheat and barley fell to women. According to one school of historians, it was women who discovered that, from the patches of ground where they dropped seeds of wild wheat, more wheat would sprout the following year – a discovery that is said to have laid the foundations of civilization.

Today's industrial farming is often a man's business. Even on the smaller-scale farms that dominate in developing countries, the role of women in rural areas is very often relegated to tasks such as weeding, harvesting, or ferrying food and water to the male workforce. This is particularly true in the rural areas of many predominantly Muslim countries, where a woman's primary role is to look after the needs of her family and where acquiring knowledge and getting an education are not seen as priorities.

But increasingly, social scientists are discovering that women in these rural areas have a greater role in agricultural decisions than is immediately obvious. This is principally because of their responsibilities in the kitchen -- essentially transforming crops into food for their families. Women who cook for their families are effectively preserving local biological diversity through their taste buds. They use traditional recipes and insist on specific ingredients for cereals, vegetables, herbs and spices. Research in several villages in Morocco has shown that women have made it their business to acquire the kind of expert-level knowledge that in universities is called agricultural science.

One of these villages is called Tabia, which lies in the oasis of Morocco's High Ziz valley. Tabia is home to the Chorfa people. The singular for Chorfa is Cherif and it is derived from the Arabic word for 'respected.' The Chorfa claim descent from the prophet Muhammad through his daughter Fatima. Here, strict social norms dictate that women do not leave their households. This is partly why women do not participate in any agricultural work; they rarely visit the fields and many have never set foot inside a school. Yet despite this the women of Tabia and other villages in the Atlas mountains have become somewhat expert in many areas of agriculture – including irrigation; soil fertility; how to optimize yields; what determines the price of seeds (or agricultural economics); and how to select the best seeds for planting.

Our knowledge of the agricultural expertise of Morocco's rural women is due largely to the pioneering efforts of Fatima Nassif, a sociologist at the Moroccan National Institute of Agricultural Research in Settat. Nassif and her colleagues have spent much of the past decade travelling to villages, getting to know the farmers, their families, and recording their knowledge of farming. One particularly innovative approach is to bring groups of rural women down from the villages to spend time in her research center, during which they interact with conventionally-trained scientists and compare their knowledge of agriculture and ecology in formal academic seminars. It is often the first time that women from villages have set foot in a city, and definitely the first time they would have entered a center for

Above: **Chorfa men rely on women's knowledge of irrigating wheat crops. Women know how much water is needed to produce flour that will make the best bread.**

learning and research. The results are electrifying to watch.

Nassif says she has learned that women are intimately involved in agriculture, even though they may not participate in much of the fieldwork. She has found that women follow farming decisions closely and are as knowledgeable as men about the prices and quality of grain sold at local markets, or souks. Beyond this, they have a greater and more specialized knowledge of how best to transform the crops into food. She says that the knowledge held among these mountain communities is often of a high quality; and she sees part of her job as helping to make the women aware (and give them the confidence to believe) that their knowledge is as good as that acquired by conventional scientists in research laboratories.

Heaven's kitchen

An important motivation for acquiring detailed agricultural knowledge is undoubtedly their use of crops to make food. But, in addition, women are responsible for storing grain for next year's crop; they cultivate the hay that is used to feed cows; and they mill the flour for the family's bread. This gives them special insights into the quality of a crop and its many uses.

For example, experience has taught Tabia women the importance of knowledge about irrigation. They now advise men on the quantities of water needed to irrigate durum wheat because this is key to making the best bread. They know that when durum wheat receives more than enough water, it affects the quality of the flour. They prefer that the crop is left dry during the later stages of its growth.

Similarly, women in three villages in the High Ziz valley prefer to use what is called 'labiad,' the local variety of durum wheat because it provides a better yield of straw and grain. The ears of the plant are longer, the grain is fatter and the flour it makes is yellow. They say these qualities allow them to make good bread, couscous and mhamsa, a preparation of wheat similar to couscous but used in different dishes.

Taounate province is another region where agricultural

expertise lies mostly in the hands of women. Taounate's farms are often isolated by the surrounding mountain landscape, and agriculture is not easy. The terrain is fragmented, and difficult to access. Moreover, many of the men are not farmers and instead spend much of their time looking for other kinds of work. This is partly why women have had to shoulder many more responsibilities on the farm than they would if conditions were different, says Ahmed Birouk of the National Institute for Veterinary Agronomy in Rabat.

"We do everything," exclaims Hala, who lives in Taounate. "We pick the figs, transport them and dry them. We pick, carry and prepare olives for our families to eat. We carry everything on our backs, the wood to heat the house, the grass for the animals, the bags of seed. Our husbands try to find work and go to the neighboring region of Ktama to look for it. But they make little money. With average salaries of 40 dirhams (US$4.50) a day, they have to pay for their transportation and buy something to eat. After that, there's not much left." Caring for livestock also falls to Taounate's women, as does cutting, drying, and storing alfalfa, which is used for animal feed.

One specific example of Taounate women's knowledge is knowing which soils provide the best environment for optimizing the yield quality from different types of seeds. They advise the men on where to plant seeds, such as fava beans and lentils, because soils affect cooking times. "There are certain plots that produce fava beans and lentils that are difficult to cook," says Hala. "We know which fields they are and we tell our husbands so they don't plant these beans there. Instead, those parts of the farm are used for barley and durum wheat."

A second example is in their knowledge about the strengths and weaknesses of the varieties of durum wheat grains that are sold in the markets. In interviews with Fatima Nassif's research team, Taounate men acknowledge that they are not best placed to choose grain that will make good bread, for example, so a woman might accompany her husband when he goes to the market to stock up on durum wheat.

Women also make it their business to keep up-to-date with the market prices of crops. Birouk says that women are well aware that some traders mix local varieties with cheaper ones. "They want to pass the mixed seeds for local seed. But you can tell as soon as the seeds are planted. Immediately after mixed seed is planted, we notice the better performance of the local variety," says Radwa, another resident of Taounate.

Barley is a critical crop for farmers in Taounate because it feeds not only humans but also animals, particularly donkeys – widely used to transport humans and other animals such as poultry. However, barley grown on family farms is often not enough to meet these needs and families have to purchase additional quantities in the local market. Once more, it is Taounate's women, rather than men, who know the difference between different barley varieties, and their respective strengths and weaknesses.

A job for government

Most of Morocco's agriculture comes from the plains and the majority of farmers do not produce on an industrial scale. This is something that the government, like many in the developing world, is keen to change. For example, it wants to introduce modern methods of production and management – including more use of farm machinery – so that farmers can grow large quantities of higher-yielding crops, which they can sell. At the same time, the government is also attracted to genetic modification in agriculture, particularly the development of crops whose genetic makeup can be modified to make them resist drought, or salinity, or produce greater yields.

What do Morocco's mountain farmers make of this? The answer is that they have yet to be convinced. They know, for example, that many of the new varieties of seeds will not be suited to the soils and atmosphere of mountain regions. The seeds that farmers cultivate in the mountains have been planted and crossed with others for generations, yielding hardy plants that can resist the difficult mountainous environments and adapt to year-on-year changes. These seeds will produce good hay, good grain and, ultimately, tasty, nutritious food.

That is not to say that Morocco's mountain farmers have no use for the products of modern science. What they benefit from is advice on how to conserve the many different species used in agriculture and how to make this available to farmers so that they never run out. Morocco, for example, desperately needs what is known as a genebank, a national store of all of Morocco's known seeds, catalogued and available to any farmer or plant breeder who is running low on supplies.

Morocco is a party to several international treaties and conventions on protecting its natural environment, including the UN Convention on Biological Diversity, the Global Plan of Action for the Conservation and Sustainable Use of Plant Genetic Resources for Food and Agriculture, and the Commission on Genetic Resources for Food and Agriculture. But it has no national strategy for conserving its crops and no one knows precisely which species are in use or how many species are disappearing, either through neglect, or over-use. What needs to happen is a systematic effort to combine the knowledge of scientists with that of the women in Morocco's villages – and then make the results available to both.

The true keepers of Morocco's biological diversity, believes Nassif, are the farmers, particularly women because they are involved not just in the production of crops but also in the way crops are transformed into food for humans and livestock. Their understanding of farming is more 'holistic' and practical, incorporating detailed knowledge of how the plants are grown, used, stored and sold.

The UN Convention on Biological Diversity recognizes the role of women in the conservation and use of biological resources and the importance of involving them in all aspects of policymaking. This makes a great deal of sense. It was women after all, who invented the art of growing seed.

Catherine Brahic is a staff journalist for the Science and Development Network and is based in London. Some names have been changed.

Oman's rose gardens

by Mike Shanahan

In the mountains of Oman, communities have produced a prized rose essence based on ancient ingenuity for centuries. Now threats to a precious resource could wither the gardens they depend on.

"Live near water and ask not about sustenance."

So goes an Omani proverb. And for the rose growers of Oman's Saiq plateau, it is good advice. Every April, the air there is full of the fragrance of pink roses all thanks to ancient ingenuity that lets water flow year-round.

The plateau – 2,000 meters above sea level in the Jebel Akhdar mountains near the Arabian Peninsula's southeastern tip – receives more rain than anywhere else in northern Oman. But at just 300 millimeters a year, there is precious little to spare. Nevertheless, rose bushes bloom abundantly on terraces carved out of the rock, their petals feeding an industry little changed for centuries. The cultivation of these gardens – and indeed, human life – is only possible here because, one to two millennia ago, local people began creating a system of covered channels to carry water to the villages and fields.

This irrigation system has allowed societies to blossom alongside the roses and other crops, and has helped determine the special blend of species that share the region.

Previous page: A profusion of highly scented rose petals lie heaped and ready for Oman's rosewater distilleries.

Opposite: Fed by falaj: Balad Seet, an oasis in the rose-growing regions of Oman's Jebal Akhdar mountains, boasts terraces and a traditional falaj irrigation system more than 2,500 years old.

Mountain of marvels

Jebel Akhdar is Arabic for 'green mountain' – a reference to both the hue of the local limestone, and the groves of wild olives and juniper trees that dot the slopes. Thanks in part to painstaking research from Reginald Victor, Professor of Biology and Director of the Centre for Environmental Studies and Research at Sultan Qaboos University in Oman, we know that the mountains of northern Oman, which rise to some 3,000 meters, are home to nearly two-thirds of the country's 1,200 plant species. Animals living there include the Arabian tahr (*Hemitragus jayakari*), a wild mountain goat found only in northern Oman and the neighboring United Arab Emirates, and at least 70 bird species, including the rare lappet-faced vulture (*Torgos tracheliotus*).

Among the dramatic peaks and plunging valleys more than 50 small villages perch precariously on clifftops. Until recently, the only way in was by donkey, helicopter or on foot.

The pace of life in these villages is slow. Traditions there

have been relatively untouched by modernity, and for centuries, the villagers of Shuraijah and Al Ayn have tended roses in their upland gardens. Each year, for a few weeks in March and April, they gather at dawn to pluck the biggest petals. In household distilleries called *al dhujan*, the villagers boil the petals in clay pots sealed within a hearth of hot coals. The vapors condense into a metal container in the pot. Once cooled, this residue is filtered to yield a liquid called rosewater.

Unlike the clear rosewater produced in the West with modern equipment, the traditionally distilled Omani rosewater is brown and smoky-scented. The process also yields small quantities of rose oil, which floats on top of the rosewater. This is called *attar* (in English, 'attar of roses,' from an old Persian word meaning "to smell sweet"). You encounter this scent throughout Oman. Rosewater is an essential ingredient there in coffee and sweets such as *halwa*, and is used to perfume houses during weddings and Islamic ceremonies. It is also used as a local remedy for headaches and stomach pain.

Some cosmetics manufacturers are also enamored of Oman's rosewater and *attar*. In the 1980s, Guy Robert, a French master perfumer, used rose oil and water from Jebel Akhdar – along with 120 other ingredients, including Omani frankincense – to create Amouage, one of the world's most expensive perfumes.

As so often happens with highly successful, but small-scale traditional industries, the pressure to modernize and produce on a larger scale is never far away. Yet so far, the 100 or so essence extractors working in Jebel Akhdar have rejected modern distillery equipment in favor of their time-tested approach, which they say produces the highest-quality rosewater. This special technique and reputation, along with the roses' short flowering season, make Omani rosewater the costliest in local markets, where demand outstrips supply.

That is not to say that the industry in its present form is unprofitable. Far from it. Each rose bush produces up to 20 kilograms of petals – enough for just ten 750-milliliter bottles of rosewater, which sell for about 5 rials (US$13) each. From picking the flowers to the final product, entire households are

involved, and some families in Jebel Akhdar earn 6,000 rials (US$15,600) a year from the industry. Oman's GDP per capita in 2004 was, at US$13,100, noticeably less than this.

But rosewater's value is more than just monetary. It also has social cachet, and is often presented as a gift to distant relatives and highly regarded guests.

When the rose growing season is over, the farmers of Jebel Akhdar turn their attention to their orchards. They sell excess produce such as apricots, peaches, pomegranates, almonds and walnuts in the markets of Nizwa and other nearby towns. This lifestyle is made possible by the ancient *falaj* irrigation system, which uses a network of tunnels and covered channels to ensure a year-round supply of water.

Above: **On the scent: in *al dhujan* or domestic distilleries, villagers in Jebel Akhdar gather and inspect the petals (top) and (bottom) boil them in clay pots to condense the vapors, producing precious rosewater and rose oil.**

Ancient ingenuity

Some *falaj* tunnels tap water locked away underground in porous rock, but most of those in Jebel Akhdar draw water from *wadi* streams or natural springs.

"The water is close to the soil surface and seeps out naturally," says Abdullah Al-Ghafri, a researcher in the Department of Soils, Water and Agricultural Engineering at Sultan Qaboos University in Muscat. "The excavated canals or 'cut-and-covered' tunnels bring this water to areas that need it. These systems can be dated to the early Iron Age – before 1,000 BC." Indeed, the world's oldest known *falaj*, recently excavated in the United Arab Emirates by archaeologist Walid Yasin Al-Tikriti, was built more than 3,000 years ago.

The system was introduced to Oman between one and two millennia ago, and there are about 3,000 operating in the country, most more than 1,000 years old. Long thought to have originated in ancient Persia before spreading through the Middle East and beyond, recent archaeological evidence suggests that the technique is of Arabic origin.

Oman's Awamir tribe is especially renowned for its skill at finding springs or underground water, and building a *falaj* to tap them. They divine water by examining the soil, and looking for particular plants growing in the area.

The ancient *falaj* builders would dig a gently sloping tunnel up from the village where the water was needed to the meet the source. Too steep a slope, and the water would rush too quickly through the tunnel, eroding it and causing sections to collapse. The low gradient – typically 1:500 to 1:2,500 – means the tunnels can stretch for up to 15 kilometers.

The first *falaj* builders could have created above-ground aqueducts, but evaporation would rapidly diminish the vital resource. Keeping the water underground meant a lot more work, but left enough to use. Al-Ghafri, who has been studying Oman's *falaj* systems for about a decade, says that creating them required ingenuity and bravery, as the work was both technically challenging and dangerous. "Being underground in a limited space with extreme temperature and humidity, as well as a heavy

workload, meant facing death at any moment," he says. "Excavating hundreds of tonnes of soil using simple tools, the workers were threatened by suffocation, dehydration, reptile and insect bites, and collapsing tunnels."

"That they made systems that survived for hundreds of years, using very simple tools to dig in hard stone, measure the slope of the tunnels and then line the tunnels, is really outstanding," adds Al-Ghafri.

Sharing the wealth

In Jebel Akhdar, the tunnels emerge as lined channels and snake overland, hugging the contours of the mountainsides or the walls

of cliffs. To minimize evaporation and pollution, they are often covered with slabs. In places, these covered channels are also the sole path along mountain ledges.

The real beauty of the *falaj* system is that it relies on gravity – there is nothing mechanical that could break down, and the water is transported for free. But this also means that the water flows constantly, day and night. If it is not carefully managed, it will be wasted.

In relatively small *falaj* systems, such of those of Jebel Akhdar, water flows down the main tunnel to a storage chamber. From there, a network of overland channels direct the water first to areas for domestic use – drinking, bathing, washing dishes and clothes – and finally, through another network of channels, to the fields. The water for home use and watering animals is freely available, but the right to irrigate crops with *falaj* water is tightly controlled.

The villagers use a sundial to mark the passage of the allotted time. When that elapses, the *falaj* overseer uses a piece of stone or wood to divert the water into the channel serving the next plot of land. Nor does this timeshare system end when the sun sets. At night, the movement of stars is used to schedule the sharing of the water.

The *falaj* system is usually administered by a committee of elders headed by a *wakil* (representative), who coordinates ownership of rights over *falaj* water and decides when to use revenues raised in the auctions to repair the channels. But it is only by division of labor that a *falaj* can be made and maintained. The systems became the foundations for farming communities, as a stable water supply allowed permanent, self-sufficient settlements to establish in this isolated, drought-prone region. Having water meant more land could be cultivated and a greater variety of crops grown.

Wild species also benefit. The villagers' fields and orchards provide a lush habitat for insects, birds and lizards. The open *falaj* channels support dragonflies and toads. "Plant species in Oman are very well adapted to the dry desert conditions, so one really cannot say that they benefit from the *falaj* systems," says Shahina Ghazanfar of the Royal Botanic Gardens at Kew in

Opposite: **Clouds of pink roses throng the terraced slopes above the Saiq Plateau in the Jebel Akhdar.**

London, UK. "But those species growing next to the channels do much better – and there are some species which grow only there, such as some mosses and algae that require permanent moisture."

The system is self-regulating: when the flow declines in times of drought, the *falaj* committee can decide which gardens should receive water first. Unlike wells, a *falaj* system cannot exhaust the water table it taps. "That's why these systems survived for hundreds of years," says Al-Ghafri.

A dying art?

The *falaj* system is not just the network of channels – it is a way of life. It is common for Omani farmers, upon meeting, to enquire about the state of the *falaj* channels. "God willing, they are full," is the traditional response.

But the future of Jebel Akhdar's *falaj* systems, and thus its rosewater farmers, hangs in the balance. Although the channels were built with basic tools, the expertise behind the engineering took centuries to develop. More than a millennium ago, Muhammad Ibn Al-Hasan Al-Hasib Al-Khariji published methods of calculating how to dig the tunnels in his book *Inbat al miyah al khafiyah* (*Extracting the Hidden Water*).

Today, however, fewer than 200 members of the Awamir tribe retain the knowledge of traditional *falaj* construction techniques. When Oman discovered and began producing oil in the 1960s, the ancient water channels suddenly seemed, to many, deeply irrelevant. With migration away from Jebel Akhdar increasing, the *falaj* systems are falling into disrepair. Many have been abandoned.

More than a quarter of the systems in Oman are now classified as 'dead,' says Al-Ghafri, adding that the last time any were constructed in Jebel Akhdar was between the 1960s and 1980s. He adds that today, many farmers do not even know the location of the water source their *falaj* faucets.

By 1995, the government of Oman was installing water-harvesting ponds and boreholes with which to tap underground water near most villages, says Martin Hollingham of the Centre for Arid Zone Studies at the University of Bangor in the UK. The country's agriculture and fisheries ministry provided subsidies to encourage farmers to take up the new techniques. But between 1994 and 2003, the government also spent millions of rials repairing about 1,000 *falaj* systems, setting up a special department to do this work and additional research on the water resources feeding the channels, as well as demand for them.

A delicate balance

According to the UN Food and Agriculture Organization, Oman faces an imminent water crisis. Much of the country is classed as sub-tropical desert. There are no permanent streams and almost all agriculture is irrigated. But demand is set to rise. The Syrian-based Arab Center for the Studies of Arid Zones and Dry Lands predicts that Oman's annual need for water – which in 1985 was 500 million cubic meters – would increase to 7,500 million cubic meters by 2025.

The ancient legacy of Oman's *falaj* systems could play a central role in ensuring that the traditions of Jebel Akhdar, from rose farming to clever engineering, persist into the future – along with the region's precious natural heritage, its biodiversity. "The *falaj* systems have lasted for hundreds of years in harmony with the surrounding environment, and is of central economic and cultural importance to life in the villages and ecology of northern Oman," says Al-Ghafri. "If the *aflaj* were abandoned, the local environment would suffer and thousands of farmers who depend on them would lose their way of life."

"In any traditional system, people oppose modernization," he says. "The challenge is to adapt to the future while preserving the character of the past."

Above: **Bottled bliss: vessels containing *attar* of roses from Jebel Akhdar crowd a stall in Muttrak Souk, Muscat, Oman. Some families earn up to US$15,600 a year from the industry.**

Mike Shanahan is News Editor at the Science and Development Network, and is based in London

Author biographies

Editor biographies

Ehsan Masood is a science writer based in London and Project Director of The Gateway Trust (www.gatewaytrust.org). He is a former Director of Communications of LEAD International and has worked as an editor on *New Scientist* magazine and a writer on the weekly journal *Nature*. He is the author of *Who Decides?*, an introduction to the politics of genetically-modified food in developing countries (Panos, 2005).

Daniel Schaffer is the Public Information Officer at the Academy of Sciences for the Developing World (www.twas.org), based in Trieste. He has written and edited several books including *Conserving Biodiversity in Arid Regions* (Kluwer Academic Press, 2003) and *Garden Cities for America* (Temple University Press, 1982). He has also written and produced documentary films and has a PhD in history from Rutgers University, USA.

Contributor biographies

Aleem Ahmed is the founder and Editor-in-Chief of *Global Science*, a mass-circulation monthly published in Urdu out of Karachi. He is a former editor of a second popular science magazine in Urdu, called *Science Digest*.

Adnan Badran is the Former Prime Minister of the Hashemite Kingdom of Jordan. A trained biochemist he led Jordan's Ministry of Agriculture and is a former Deputy Director General of the United Nations Educational, Scientific and Cultural Organization (UNESCO), based in Paris.

Pallava Bagla is the award-winning Chief South Asia Correspondent with the weekly journal *Science*, and is based in New Delhi. A Fellow of Leadership for Environment and Development he is the author (with Subhadra Menon) of *Trees of the Indian subcontinent* (Odyssey, 1999).

John Bohannon contributes articles on science in the Middle East for the weekly journal *Science*. He has a PhD in molecular biology from the University of Oxford and is writing a comedy musical about human cloning.

Catherine Brahic is a writer and journalist for the Science and Development Network (www.SciDev.Net), an online news agency reporting on science in developing countries. She reports on climate change, science policy, infectious diseases and sustainable development.

Nadia El-Awady is the award-winning Health and Science Editor at the Internet portal *IslamOnline.Net*, based in Cairo. She chairs the program committee of the World Federation of Science Journalists.

Jim Giles is a news and features writer for the weekly science journal *Nature*, based in London. His specialist areas include the science and politics of global environment and development issues.

Mohamed Hassan is the Executive Director of the Academy of Sciences for the Developing World (TWAS) and Secretary General of the Third World Network of Scientific Organizations. A mathematician by training he is also President of the African Academy of Sciences.

Jia Hepeng is a science correspondent with the Beijing-based *China Daily* and is Regional Coordinator for China for the Science and Development Network. He is the translator of a book, *The Ruling Class* (Nanjing, 2002).

Robert Koenig is an award-winning science writer based in South Africa and a contributor to the weekly journal, *Science*. His first book, *The Fourth Horseman*, will be published by Public Affairs Press in 2006.

Marcelo Leite is a science writer in São Paulo, Brazil. He has written 6 popular books on biotechnology and environment themes. He also writes a weekly science column for the daily *Folha de S. Paulo* and publishes the blog, *Ciência em Dia*.

Peter McGrath is a science writer and editor with the Academy of Sciences for the Developing World in Trieste, Italy. He has a PhD in disease epidemiology from the University of Leeds, UK

Katie Mantell is a writer and editor based in London specializing in science and healthcare. She has worked as a journalist in Santiago, Chile, and is a former editor at the Science and Development Network.

Yvonne Ndege is a journalist with BBC television news, based in London and is a producer on the nightly current affairs programme Newsnight. She also writes for the *Daily Nation* of Kenya.

Fred Pearce is a London-based writer and broadcaster on environmental science and consultant to *New Scientist* magazine. The author of many books, his two latest titles are: *When The Rivers Run Dry*, on the global water crisis, and *The Last Generation* on climate change.

C.N.R. Rao is President of the Academy of Sciences for the Developing World (TWAS) and the Third World Network of Scientific Organizations (TWNSO). He chairs the Scientific Advisory Committee to the Prime Minister of India.

Mike Shanahan is News Editor at the Science and Development Network. He has a PhD in rainforest ecology from the University of Leeds, UK.

Liu Weifeng is a health and environment correspondent with *China Daily* based in Beijing. She was runner-up in the 2005 Developing Asia Journalism Awards. She is also the author of a guide to tourism in China.

Suhail Yusuf is the Editor of the Urdu monthly *Global Science* and is a frequent contributor to radio and television in Pakistan.

Further reading

General
Conserving biodiversity in arid regions: best practices in developing nations edited by John Lemmons, Daniel Schaffer and Reginald Victor (Kluwer Academic Press, 2003).

Sharing innovative experiences: examples of the conservation and sustainable use of dryland biodiversity (United Nations Development Programme, 2004). Free to download from http://tcdc.undp.org/experiences/vol9/content9new.asp.

Science and Development Network, an online resource on science and technology in developing countries. Free to access from http://www.scidev.net.

Brazil
Hidden view: images of Bahia, Brazil by Amanda Hopkinson (Colporteur publishers, 1994)

Burkina Faso
At the desert's edge: oral histories from the Sahel by Nigel Cross and Rhiannon Barker (Panos Publishing, 1994). See also http://www.panos.org.uk.

Chile
The desert diaries: 100 days across the Atacama by Elly Foote and Nathan Foote (N E Publishing, 2004).

China
Practice of sustainable development in China by Li Lailai (Leadership for Environment and Development, 2002). See also www.lead.org.

Egypt
The global status of the corncrake by Norbert Schaffer and Rhys Green (Royal Society for the Protection of Birds, 2001). Free to download from http://www.corncrake.net

India
Making water everybody's business: practice and policy of water harvesting (Centre for Science and Environment (www.cseindia.org). See also http://www.tarunbharatsangh.org; and the Honeybee Network of local innovators in India at http://www.sristi.org/honeybee.html.

Jordan
Arid land resources and their management: Jordan's desert margin by R. W. Dutton (Kegan Paul, 1998). See also http://www.rgs.org/templ.php?page=5jorbib for a comprehensive online bibliongraphy of research on the Badia region of Jordan.

Kenya
Parks beyond parks: genuine community-based wildlife ecotourism or just another loss of land for Maasai pastoralists in Kenya? by Marcel Rutten (International Institute for Environment and Development, 2002). See also http://www.iied.org and the National Museums of Kenya at http://www.museums.or.ke.

Mexico
Future challenges of managing a threatened global resource: the case of fresh water sustainability in west central Mexico (Leadership for Environment and Development, 2004). Free to download from http://casestudies.lead.org

Morocco
Communities and the environment: ethnicity, gender and the state in community based conservation, by Arun Agrawal & Clark Gibson (Rutgers University Press, 2001)

Namibia
Changing resource use in Namibia's lower Kuiseb river valley: perceptions from the Topnaar community by Andy Botelle and Kelly Kowaiski (Institute of Southern African Studies, 1999)

Nepal
Himalayan waters: promise, potential, problems and politics by Bhim Subba (Panos South Asia, 2001). See also International Centre for Integrated Mountain Development at http://www.icimod.org.

Oman
Water and tribal settlement in south-east Arabia: study of the aflaj of Oman by John Craven Wilkinson (Oxford University Press, 1977)

Pakistan
Thar: the great Pakistani desert by Ihsan H. Nadiem (Sang-e-Meel Publications, 2001). See also Baanhn Beli (Friend Forever), a non-profit organization working among the people of Thar at http://www.baanhnbeli.org.pk.

Sudan
Camel fables from the sailors of the Sudan, by Thurlow, R Weed Jr (Lightning Source UK, 2004). See also University of Khartoum at http://www.uofk.edu

Vicuña conservation
Distribution and conservation of the vicuña by H Torres (World Conservation Union, 1984). See also World Conservation Union website at http://www.iucn.org.

Index

Acknowledgements

This book would not have been possible without the vision, commitment and enthusiastic support of many institutions and individuals.

First and foremost we would like to thank the Academy of Sciences for the Developing World (TWAS) and the Third World Network of Scientific Organizations (TWNSO) in Trieste, Italy, especially Mohamed H.A. Hassan who heads both organizations. His willingness to take a risk on this project, and the confidence he has shown in the editors to pull it off, has made the project possible. We only hope that the book we have produced is worthy of his support and that we are able to reach out to a larger audience on an issue of critical concern to both TWAS and TWNSO, which has been our goal since the project's inception. The project team would additionally like to thank the Global Environment Facility (GEF) in Washington DC; the Initiative on Science and Technology for Sustainability (ISTS) located at Harvard University's Kennedy School of Government; the United Nations Development Programme's (UNDP) Special Unit for South-South Cooperation (SSC) in New York City; the United Nations Educational, Scientific and Cultural Organization (UNESCO) in Paris; the World Meteorological Organization (WMO) in Geneva; and Leadership for Environment and Development (LEAD) in London – all of which, in one way or another, have helped us build the roster of case studies on which the articles in the book are based.

Special thanks also go to Peter Tallack of the London literary agency Conville and Walsh who was instrumental in developing the concept; David Dickson, founding director of the Science and Development Network (www.scidev.net), one the world's leading source of news, comment, information and home for some of the best writers on science and development; Michael Fisher, inspirational editor-in-chief of Harvard University Press, for his commitment to the book and for his editorial suggestions; and the reviewers for their many constructive comments.

And last, but not least, thanks go to the hundreds of men and women living in the dry regions that are featured in this book. This book – indeed the project of which it is a part – would not have been possible without your stories, experiences, and knowledge of life without water. Thank you.

Photographic Acknowledgements

Grateful acknowledgement is made to the following sources and photographers for permission to reproduce their photographs on the following pages:

Abdullah Al-Ghafri: 14, 183
Majd Al-Hammoud: 157
Art Directors and Trip: 16,18, 20-21, 23, 25, 60, 70, 142, 154, 166, 171, 173 (Helene Rogers); 17 (David Clegg); 26 (Warren Jacobs); 36 (Ask Images); 37 (B.Ross); 48 (R.Cracknell); 51 (B.Vikander); 52 (Robin Smith); 80; 98 (Judy Drew); 105 (Chris Rennie); 110 (Jane Sweeney); 120 (University of Essex); 130 (T.Bognar); 167, 168 (M. Jelliffe); 176, 187 (Juliet Highet) **Baanhn Belli**, Pakistan: 83, 85, 89 top, middle, bottom **Badia Research and Development Centre**: 158, 160-161, 165 right **Pallava Bagla**: 73, 74, 75, 77, 79 **CNS Photo**: 61, 67 **Nadia El-Awady**: 143, 146, 147, 151 **FLPA**: 43 (Patricia Fogden/Minden Pictures); 49 (Terry Andrewartha) 71 (Cyril Ruoso/JH Editorial/Minden); 121 (SA Team/Foto Natura); 122-123 (Patricia Robles Gil/Sierra Madre/Minden); 126 (Michael & Patricia Fogden/Minden); 128 (Jurgen & Christine Sohns); 152 (Michael Callan) **Ann Furr**: 11, 163, 165 left **Shahina A. Ghazanfar**: 181 top right, bottom right, bottom left; 184 **IUCN Pakistan**: 8, 86, 88 **Ibrahim Khader**: 155, 156 **Marcelo Leite**: 111, 112, 114, 115, 117, 118, 119 **Alfred Limbrunner**: 144 **Mountain Camera**: 90, 91, 92 top and bottom, 94, 95 (John Cleare); 93, 96 (Colin Monteath) **Nature Picture Library**: 5 (Bernard Castelein); 56-57 (Anup Shah); 132, 169 (Chris Gomersall); 134, 138 top, middle , bottom, 139 (Pete Oxford);177, 179, 181 top left (Hanne & Jens Eriksen) **Newsphoto China**: 64, 65, 66 **Panos Pictures**: 27, 28, 30, 31, 35 (Jeremy Hartley); 81 (Neil Cooper); 131 (Stefan Boness); 175 (Penny Tweedy) **Still Pictures**: endpapers, 99, 102, 106-107 (Gil Moti); 34 top (Mark Edwards); 38 top and bottom (C.Danni/I.Jeske); 39, 41, 44-45, 47 (Frans Lemmens); 59 (M.&C. Denis-Huot); 55 (Muriel Nicolotti); 125 (Gary Braasch); 133 (Gunter Zieslar); 174 (Thierry Thomas) **Tree Aid**: 13, 33, 34 bottom **Li Xinrong**: 69